REMEMBERING KERNERSVILLE

REMEMBERING KERNERSVILLE

Michael L. Marshall
& Jerry L. Taylor

THE History PRESS

Published by The History Press
Charleston, SC 29403
www.historypress.net

Front Cover: painting by Mildred Ballard, courtesy of Barbara Bull.
Back Cover: bottom left: Korner's Folly, courtesy of Wayne Biby; right: tavern, *Kernersville Bicentennial Book*, 1976.

First published 2010

Manufactured in the United States

ISBN 978.1.60949.115.4

Library of Congress Cataloging-in-Publication Data

Marshall, Michael L. (Michael Lee), 1944-
Remembering Kernersville / Michael L. Marshall and Jerry L. Taylor.
p. cm.
Includes bibliographical references.
ISBN 978-1-60949-115-4
1. Kernersville (N.C.)--History--Anecdotes. 2. Kernersville (N.C.)--Biography--Anecdotes.
I. Taylor, Jerry L. (Jerry Lee), 1937- II. Title.
F264.K45M37 2010
975.6'67--dc22
2010043533

This book is dedicated to our parents, Lee J. and Nell (Stafford) Marshall and George Willis and Mozelle (Tatum) Taylor.

Contents

Contents

Preface

Uncovering previously unknown facts about the history of Kernersville has become both a passion and a pleasure for us. But after a few years of accumulating material, it seemed that we should try and organize our findings in a way that would allow us to share them with a larger public.

A couple of years ago, we tried that, and the result was a book about some of the town's more exciting moments from its early days. We called it *Wicked Kernersville: Rogues, Robbers, Ruffians & Rumrunners*. When it appeared in April 2009, we anticipated some negative reaction from a descendant or two whose ancestors might have been involved in one of the dust-ups described in the book. On the contrary, we had people tell us they bought the book hoping to find a wicked ancestor lurking in its pages. Not only that, but readers also came forward to share material on events in the book that were new to us. We only wished we had it when we were writing the book.

As you might imagine, all this encouraged us to try our hand at another volume, and this is the result. It is a collection of stories about people, places and events that are also part of the town's historical fabric. It is an eclectic compilation, as the reader will soon discover.

The Kernersville of today is not the town we knew growing up. Then, it was a small mill town where many of the residents were related through either blood or marriage. Now, more than one-third of its inhabitants were born outside North Carolina. Interestingly, these "come-heres" seem highly motivated to learn something of their adopted residence. We trust this book will help them in their quest. We also hope it will convince some of the "been-heres" that when it comes to their town's history, there is something new under the sun.

Acknowledgements

The list of people we need to thank for helping us bring this book into being is long. Janelle Warden shared her research on the Morrow family. Tom Parker provided information on his ancestor, William Dobson, a prominent Kernersville historical fixture. Dennis Feltgen, public affairs officer at the National Hurricane Center in Miami, Florida, generously gave us permission to use material from the National Oceanic and Atmospheric Administration website as illustrations. Robert Sears, director of Library Services at Southern Wesleyan University, kindly shared his knowledge of the educational facilities the former Pilgrim Holiness Church once maintained in Kernersville. We are also grateful for the information Garland Burns Porter Jr. and his wife, Lee, shared with us on William Porter, who was both a Methodist minister and, later, an attorney in Kernersville—quite a combination. Cam Steel shared his findings on the American Hosiery Mill. Leroy Wagner made a drawing of the Beard & Roberts tobacco factory from an old photo shared by John Wolfe and kindly gave us permission to use it. While we were writing our sketch on the Northwestern North Carolina Railroad, the first line to run through Kernersville, Alan Coleman and Matt Bumgarner were most helpful. Alan is the author of the book *Railroads of North Carolina*. Wayne Biby and Clarke Stephens have extensive tobacco memorabilia and postcard collections and allowed us to copy some of their Kernersville-related material for the book. Also, thanks to Dave Teague, a Quaker historian, for his contributions to our Muddy Creek story.

As the reader will see, Gloria Lowrey proved to be a wonderful source for old photos of Kernersville, as were many others who were also gracious in letting us use photographic material from their collections. They included Edgar Shore Jr., Richard B. Edwards, the children of Samuel F. Vance Jr., members of the Mary Ruth Körner family, the Ellen Cook family, the Hull family, Nettie Hester, Nell Marshall, Terry Motsinger, Robert U. Stuart and Mildred Weavil.

Thanks also to Jessica Berzon of The History Press for her help in getting this project off the ground. Likewise, thanks to all the other History Press professionals who saw it to its conclusion—thanks Jess and everyone else there in Charleston.

Getting History Off on the Wrong Foot

Legends die hard in America, and that is certainly the case for the one surrounding the first pioneer to acquire land in what is now Kernersville, North Carolina. For more than 120 years, traditional accounts have credited a man named Caleb Story as being the first settler, despite historical evidence that it was actually a Scots-Irish pioneer named David Morrow. So, if the facts don't support this story, how did the town's history get off on the wrong foot?

Historical sleuthing has turned up evidence that Thomas Early Whitaker was the gentleman who launched the Caleb Story legend. In his early days, Whitaker, staff correspondent for the *Durham Recorder*, penned a sketch of Kernersville that was reprinted in the January 13, 1888 edition of the *News & Farm*, a Kernersville newspaper. In it, Whitaker wrote:

> *Kernersville is one hundred and twenty years old. It was first settled about the year 1760 by Caleb Story, an Irishman. Tradition says that he bought the original tract of 400 acres, in which the town was built, for four gallons of rum. He sold to Dobson, and for many years the town was known by the unpretentious name, "Dobson's X Roads." Dobson sold to Schober, and Schober to Joseph Kerner, a native of Germany, in 1818, who bought additional tracts to the amount of 1,100 acres.*

Where Whitaker got his story is unknown—an earlier, 1878, account of the town's origins does not mention Story. Whitaker did have Kernersville

Circa 1909 postcard view of Kernersville's Main Street looking north from the town square. *Courtesy of Wayne Biby.*

connections and may have picked it up from one of them. Regardless, Whitaker's version likely would have had little historical impact had it not been for another event that occurred a few months after its appearance.

As it turned out, the Winston-Salem Chamber of Commerce had commissioned a gentleman named Dr. David Peter Robbins to produce a book on the twin city and its environs aimed at attracting new business and investment to the area, and Robbins also included a sketch of Kernersville in it. To gather information on Kernersville, Robbins visited the town, according to a piece in the June 22, 1888 *News & Farm*:

> *Dr. Robbins has about finished the sketch of Winston-Salem and will be here the first part of next week to gather information for the article on Kernersville. The Doctor has sent us advance pages of more than half the work, which we shall be pleased to show to any one who will call at our office, and which speaks higher in his praise as a skillful writer and compiler than a column of encomiums from us could do. We are much obliged to Dr. Robbins and to the Committee of the Chamber of Commerce, who have kindly consented to give Kernersville a representation in this worthy work and we trust that the generosity of our citizens will fully repay them for the trouble and space required to give us a proper representation.*

Given these events, and the similarities between the Whitaker and Robbins pieces, it seems certain that Robbins was made aware of Whitaker's earlier sketch during his visit to Kernersville. Indeed, Robbins's account is nearly identical to Whitaker's:

> *About the year 1760 this nearly level plateau, upon the county's water shed, was selected by Caleb Story, an Irishman, who, it is said bought 400 acres for four gallons of rum. A few years later Story sold his interest to a Mr. Dobson, the place for many years being known as Dobson's Cross Roads. Rev. Gottlieb Schober, of Salem, purchased this homestead in 1806 for his son Nathaniel and the Schobers sold to Joseph Kerner in 1817, from whom the place takes its name.*

Dr. Robbins's work was widely circulated at the time and almost surely was used as a reference in yet another account of how the town originated that appeared in print in 1898. It was written by the well-known chronicler of the Moravians in North Carolina, Dr. Adelaide Fries. Other versions appeared in several subsequent books, including one in 1924 by Charles Siewers and another by Fries in a 1949 book prepared as part of the celebration of the 100th anniversary of Forsyth County, which was formed in 1849. Jules Gilmer Körner Jr. also described the town's evolution in his 1958 volume, *Joseph of Kernersville*. His version also echoed earlier ones as regards Caleb Story.

A more recent narrative can be found in a book prepared for the town's bicentennial celebration staged in 1971. Aptly called the *Kernersville Bicentennial Book*, this largely pictorial history provides this highly embroidered version:

> *And now, at last, Kernersville's first hero makes his appearance on history's slate. His name was Caleb Story and he is described as an Irishman, but he was probably Scotch-Irish (which as any Scotsman will tell you is a different thing altogether). At any rate he came walking or riding along a high ridge two hundred miles from the sea and nearly a thousand feet above sea level…Perhaps he had never owned an acre in the old world but now in the year of our Lord 1756, or thereabouts, he, Caleb Story, had a land grant from the Royal Colony of Carolina for this strip of land…At some time during this period Caleb Story sold his land to one, David Morrow, whose name indicates he was Irish (or Scotch-Irish) too…About the year 1771 our third hero, William Dobson, an emigrant from Ireland, bought*

the land from David Morrow. William Dobson must have been a man of means, a solid and respected citizen. He was a Justice of the Peace and is also referred to as "Captain Dobson." His son William P. Dobson was elected a representative from our county to the State Assembly on August 11, 1814. After his original purchase of the land, William Dobson bought other tracts of land adjoining the original four hundred acres until the tract contained 1133 acres.

For whatever reasons, it seems each of these authors was content merely to recount versions of the original Whitaker narrative crediting Caleb Story as the first settler, when the actual record would have provided a historically accurate chronicle.

But what about Caleb Story? Yes, he existed and he did own one of the six tracts of land later acquired by Joseph Kerner. However, he did not receive his 125-acre State of North Carolina land grant until November 29, 1797, and he sold it to William Dobson on February 28, 1801.

Circa 1930 view of Kernersville's Main Street looking north from the town square. *Courtesy of Gloria Lowrey.*

Dobson, too, acquired part of the land sold to Kerner as state land grants—the first one for fifty acres on July 9, 1794, and the others for two hundred acres and fifty-seven acres, both on December 19, 1803. Dobson also owned earlier grants in what became Kernersville that he had acquired in 1788 from David Morrow.

Tom Whitaker, who kicked off the Caleb Story legend, eventually settled in Oak Ridge, North Carolina, where in 1914 he succeeded Martin H. Holt and his brother J. Allen Holt, who had been co-principals at the Oak Ridge Institute. Whitaker reorganized the school after a fire in 1914 and eventually transformed it into a military school called Oak Ridge Military Institute. In fact, Whitaker had been associated with this institution for more than forty years, coming to it first as a student. Professor Whitaker died in March 1929. An account of his death that appeared in the March 21, 1929 edition of the *Danville Bee* noted that he had been born in Person County some sixty-three years earlier. His wife was Miss Ida Ogburn. Professor Whitaker was the father of Dr. Richard Whitaker, a well-known Kernersville physician, and brother to Frances Whitaker, who married J.R. Blackwell Sr. of Kernersville. He was the father of J.R. Blackwell Jr., longtime principal of Kernersville High School and husband to Maxine Blackwell, for many years a highly respected Kernersville public school music teacher at Kernersville and director of the choir at Main Street United Methodist Church. It is doubtful Professor Whitaker intended to launch a legend in 1888 when he wrote his essay on Kernersville, and he probably would be surprised if he were alive today to find his words still being echoed.

David Morrow, Kernersville's First Settler

As previously noted, most accounts have claimed that Caleb Story was the first white man to own land in what is now Kernersville. This is incorrect. The first landowner here was a Scots-Irish Presbyterian from Pennsylvania named David Morrow. Morrow first appears in North Carolina in the land records of Orange County—the portion that became western Guilford when that county was formed from Orange in 1771. These records state that on August 9, 1767, Morrow purchased from Herman Husband a tract of 440 acres on Buffalo Creek of Haw River, part of a grant of 640 acres made to Robert Brashears on December 6, 1761. Brashears sold the land to Husband on February 24, 1764, and he conveyed part of it to Morrow. In fact, David Morrow's wife, Martha, was a daughter of Robert Brashears. Morrow and his wife held this 440-acre tract of land until August 18, 1772, when they conveyed it to Thomas Cummings of Guilford County for the sum of £120.

It seems Morrow and many of his acquaintances were associated with what is now Buffalo Presbyterian Church in present-day Greensboro, North Carolina. This church was established in the early 1750s by a contingent of Scots-Irish settlers from West Nottingham Presbyterian Church, which was originally located in Lancaster County, Pennsylvania. That area became Cecil County, Maryland, after the Mason-Dixon survey of 1767. Many of these Scots-Irish settlers lived in the southeastern part of Lancaster County along Octorara Creek, especially in the townships of Drumore, Colerain and Little Britain.

David Morrow was one of those who left Lancaster County, Pennsylvania, and moved to Guilford County. The evidence appears in a deed made in Lancaster on November 1, 1775. In it, Anne Morrow, widow and administrator of James Morrow, deceased, of Colerain township, and David Morrow, described in the deed as a yeoman of "Guilford County in North Carolina, the only son and heir at law of the said James Morrow, deceased," conveyed to James Glenn of East Nottingham township 197 acres of land in Little Britain and Colerain Townships that had belonged to David's father, James Morrow.

In the 1770s, David and Martha Morrow moved from Guilford County into that part of Surry County that is now Forsyth. The Surry land entry books show that in August 1778, Morrow entered four hundred acres of land on the waters of Muddy Creek, Deep River, Haw River and Abotts Creek. Several years later, on November 3, 1784, Morrow received a state grant of this four-hundred-acre tract along with that for another one of two hundred acres. These grants include the heart of present-day Kernersville, where Main and Mountain Streets intersect—the so-called Cross Roads.

We know that Morrow and his wife lived somewhere on the four-hundred-acre tract. And since Morrow is often mentioned in the Surry County records in connection with roads either leading to or away from his residence, it seems likely that he and Martha may have resided at the Cross Roads itself.

On February 16, 1788, David and Martha sold their land at the Cross Roads to William Dobson. The Moravian diaries state that on September 17, 1788, a group of brothers stopped at Dobson's Tavern at noon, presumably for a meal. The fact that Dobson was operating a tavern at the Cross Roads

Circa 1920 view of Kernersville's Main Street looking south from the town square. *Courtesy of Gloria Lowrey.*

only seven months after his purchase from Morrow suggests the possibility that Morrow himself may have been operating a tavern there, but so far, no evidence to prove this has been uncovered.

After Morrow and his wife sold to Dobson, they moved back to Guilford County, where they resided for a while before moving on to Mecklenburg County, North Carolina, where land records show that on April 18, 1809, Samuel Polk conveyed to David Morrow three surveys of land for the sum of $2,500.

David Morrow must have been in declining health by February 1, 1811, the date when his son David Jr. executed a bond for $1,600 on condition that the son "tolerate the sd David Morrow, Senior, and his Wife Martha to the use of the land whereon they now live, if they may see proper, during their life time, or otherwise, if the sd David Morrow Junior…doth maintain the sd David Morrow, Senior, & his Wife Martha sufficiently on the land before named [for] both their life times." David Morrow Sr. died soon after, a fact we know because his will was proved at the May term of Mecklenburg Court in 1811. His will mentions Martha, two sons—James and David—and six daughters: Margery Higgens, Ann Crocket, Margaret, Elizabeth Pride, Martha Crocket and Jane Brown. A granddaughter, Mary K. Morrow, is also named in the will.

It appears that Martha continued to reside with her son David until her own death in either late 1832 or early 1833. Her will, dated September 1, 1830, was proved at the February term of Mecklenburg Court in 1833 but describes her as Martha Morrow "of Lancaster District," South Carolina. In fact, the Morrows had many family connections in and around the vicinity of Old Waxhaw Presbyterian Church, which is located today near the border between Lancaster County, South Carolina, and Union County, North Carolina. Old Waxhaw Presbyterian is one of the oldest churches in upcountry South Carolina, and a meetinghouse there was in use as early as 1755. Many of the Scots-Irish settlers there came from Pennsylvania and were likely friends and acquaintances of the Morrows. In fact, the Old Waxhaw Church cemetery contains the tombstone of another David Morrow engraved with the following epithet: "In memory of David Morrow who departed this life February the 18 1785 aged 54 years." The stone is surrounded by graves of members of the Crockett family, which some researchers maintain is the line of that of David or "Davy" Crockett of Tennessee, who died at the Alamo in 1836. Martha Morrow's will names her sons, David and James, several of their children and also her daughters who were then living. The children of deceased daughter Margaret were also mentioned in the will.

William Dobson and His Tavern

Kernersville is named for German immigrant Joseph Kerner, who bought land there in 1817. However, in earlier times, it was widely known as Dobson's Cross Roads after William Dobson, who began operating a tavern in 1788 at the northeast corner of present-day Main and Mountain Streets. A historical plaque marks the location today.

The tavern site was already a strategic crossroad by 1770, when it appeared on a map drawn by British cartographer John Collet. Dobson acquired the Cross Road tract from David Morrow, who held it under an original 1784 land grant from the State of North Carolina.

While Dobson figures prominently in Kernersville's early history, his origins are obscure. He may have been another of the many Scots-Irish settlers who came to the Carolina Piedmont from Pennsylvania, as did David Morrow. He first appears in a Surry County, North Carolina tax list drawn up in 1774 by Dr. Jacob Bonn, a physician in the Moravian settlements of what is now Forsyth County. Forsyth was formed from Stokes in 1849 and Stokes from Surry in 1789.

By 1776, Dobson was involved in the Revolutionary War as a captain of the local militia, taking part in the Indian war of that year against the Cherokee tribes that lived in the mountains of Virginia, North and South Carolina and Georgia. The British had incited Indian attacks against the settlers along the western frontier of these states, hoping to discourage them from joining the fight for American independence. In response, their

A winter scene from circa 1895 showing the Sapp Hotel (old Dobson's Tavern). Kernersville Bicentennial Book *photo, 1976.*

governments mounted a joint campaign against the Cherokee, striking them a devastating blow that effectively ended their participation in the war. In this campaign, General Rutherford led the North Carolina contingent, joined by Colonels Williams and Love, Major Joseph Winston and Captain William Dobson.

The affidavits of many soldiers who fought in the Revolution mention Dobson, and some refer to Dobson's Cross Roads. For example, in the March 1850 pension application of John Fields, he stated that in August 1776 his regiment "rendezvoused at Dobson's Cross Roads in the County of Surry State of N.C. now the County of Stokes," where his company became dissatisfied with Captain Deatheridge and "voted in Captain William Dobson under whom this affiant marched from that place to the Cherokee towns a distance of three hundred miles." Another former soldier, Michael Fulp, testified in March 1833 that he first entered service in a company commanded by William Dobson and William Lowe of the same unit. He added that he volunteered in the fall of 1776 for "a three months tour under the command of Captain William Dobson." David Cockerham testified in August 1832 that, during the war, his unit "marched to Fayetteville in North Carolina, and from there on to a place called Dobsons Cross Roads in Surry County, but now Stokes County by a division of the said County of Surry."

There is evidence that Dobson served as an officer of the North Carolina General Assembly about this same time. According to North Carolina's colonial and state records, his name appears in a list of members and officers of that body who received compensation for their services during the May session of 1777. Dobson was allowed £21.1.4.

Dobson's name also appears in Moravian records during this period, often as a justice of the peace. In this capacity, Dobson performed marriage ceremonies and other official duties. For example, the Bethania diary of March 19, 1777, states, "Seiler came for his certificate, and at noon he and A. Elizabeth Strub were married in the tavern by Mr. Dobson." The groom identified as Seiler was, in fact, Johannes Seiler, a name seen in later generations as Sailor or Saylor, and his bride was Anna Elizabeth Strub.

During the Revolution, many Moravians opposed taking up arms, and this caused them great difficulty. On more than one occasion, Dobson used his influence to help them. For example, the Salem diary of December 16, 1778, notes, "Peter Volz [Foltz] came from Friedberg to report that he had secured the release of his son who had been drafted, having been helped by Capt. Dobson to whom he had gone beyond Salisbury."

The Moravians also suffered because of their unwillingness to take the oath of allegiance to the new state government prescribed by the Test Act of 1775. "In case of refusal, expatriation and confiscation of property were threatened." Finally, a petition sent to the assembly meeting in Halifax, North Carolina, was favorably received, and a resolution was passed that if the Moravians would render the prescribed affirmation of fealty to North Carolina and the other states, they would be allowed to remain in possession of their property and also be exempt from all military service on condition they pay a twofold tax. Traugot Bagge, Salem merchant and spokesman for the Moravians during the Revolution, noted in his diary for 1779, "On [January] 23 [the] Assembly resolved to grant request, and later passed an act in agreement with the requirement…we made haste to take the Affirmation which was done on February 4th before Justice William Dobson in Salem and Bethania." The Salem diary of this same date adds, "About 10 o'clock Capt. Dobson arrived…Taking 20 men at a time the Captain read the Affirmation of Fidelity to this State prescribed by the Assembly on January 23, 1779…From here Captain Dobson went to Bethabara and took the Affirmation of the Brethren there." The brethren were appreciative of Dobson's efforts on their behalf in obtaining this new oath, and on February 15, 1779, they "expressed a willingness to contribute to a Douceur [gratuity] to Capt. Dobson for his trouble in taking the affirmations."

Besides his military and public service, Dobson also contributed to the war effort in other ways. The North Carolina Revolutionary army accounts note that a Committee of Claims report of November 1777 allowed Dobson £76.5.0 for "wagon and team hire" in support of local military operations. He was also a Surry County tax assessor, and an account of July 30, 1779, states that "the Assessors for the three Districts, Capt. Schmid, Capt. Dobson, Capt. Gray Bynum met in the tavern to begin their work." After Stokes County was formed from Surry, one of its tax districts was known as "Captain Dobson's" and was the one that contained the Cross Roads.

Dobson was also quite prosperous and a major landowner in and around present-day Kernersville, where he eventually acquired more than two thousand acres. He first appears in the Surry County deed books on July 18, 1778, when he entered five hundred acres of land on the middle fork of Belew's Creek, adjacent to Seth Coffin. The same day, he entered an

Circa 1910 postcard view of the Auto Inn (formerly the Sapp Hotel). *Courtesy of Wayne Biby.*

additional five hundred acres on the east side of the middle fork of Belew's Creek "then running north, joining Richard Linville's deed land, then east, then south, then west to the first station, including the place known by the name of Shepperd's Hill," a name that will be seen again later in this sketch.

On February 16, 1788, Dobson purchased two tracts of land from David Morrow, one consisting of four hundred acres and the other two hundred acres. The former contained the intersection of the two colonial roads that formed the Cross Roads itself. Dobson paid Morrow £600 for the four hundred acres of land "whereon said David Morrow now dwelleth," on the waters of Muddy Creek, Deep River, Haw River and Abbotts Creek. Clearly, Morrow and his wife, Martha (Brashears), were living on the Cross Roads tract when they conveyed it to Dobson, and they may have built the original structure Dobson converted to a tavern. This conjecture is strengthened by an entry in the Salem diary of September 17, 1788, made just a few months after Dobson's purchase, noting that several Moravian brethren stopped there: "After a hearty farewell, Br. Benzien left for Bethlehem, Pennsylvania accompanied by Br. Petersen…The Brethren Marshall, Koehler, Herbst and Br. Martin Schneider from Friedland escorted them to Dobson's Tavern where they stopped at noon."

There are many references in the Stokes County court records to William Dobson as a tavern keeper and to Dobson's Cross Roads. For example, at a court held in June 1790, the justices noted that "Capt. William Dobson has leave to keep a tavern at his dwelling house at the crossroads." A court held on March 8, 1792, also allowed that "William Dobson has leave to keep a tavern," and again, at a court held March 6, 1793, the minutes record that "William Dobson Esq. has leave to keep a tavern at his dwelling house." These entries indicate that Dobson and his wife probably resided at the tavern while they were the proprietors. The tavern itself finally appeared on a map produced in 1808 by cartographers Jonathan Price and John Strother, where the intersection is labeled "Dobson."

The Stokes County court minutes for the years 1790 to 1793 contain numerous references to roads passing to or from Dobson's to just about every other major point in the surrounding area. They mention the road from Dan River Road to William Dobson's old place to Salem; from Mr. Fry's Crossroad to the house of William Dobson on the Cross Roads; from the ridge road leading from Dobson's to the Salem Road; and from the ridge road leading to Dobson's, to list only a few.

A view of the Kernersville town square circa 1930, showing the vacant lot where Dobson's Tavern formerly stood. *Courtesy of Gloria Lowrey.*

Because of its strategic location, the Moravians frequently used the tavern during their travels. The Friedland diary of April 30, 1791, notes, "Br. Fromsch visited us today and at his request I drove to Mr. Dobson's to bring back Br. Redeken, who was taken sick on his way to Pennsylvania." But the brethren were not the only visitors to stop at Dobson's Tavern in the year 1791. Others included President George Washington and Congressman William Loughton Smith. While Washington's visit to Dobson's has been widely chronicled, Smith's is less well known but more interesting.

William Loughton Smith was born in 1758 to an affluent family in Charleston, South Carolina. He was educated in London, England, where he studied law in the Middle Temple in 1774. After returning to Charleston, he was admitted to the bar and then elected to the House of Representatives from that state, serving in the First, Second and Third Congresses. He was reelected as a Federalist to the Fourth and Fifth Congresses.

In 1791, he began a journey in Virginia that took him across the state of North Carolina and then into his home state of South Carolina. While traveling, he kept a personal journal that included his observations about the various inns, ordinaries and taverns in which he lodged and ate while on the road. His candid comments make it clear that he did not mince words in describing these hostelries or the hospitality they provided. For example, at one ordinary in Virginia he noted that "the bugs made a heartier supper on me than I did on my bacon and eggs; I was glad, however, to find that my horse fared better than I did, and before six the next morning I proceeded on my journey."

Just before crossing the Dan River from Virginia into North Carolina, Smith stopped at another wayside inn for the night. His caustic commentary about his accommodations there suggests his night was anything but restful:

> *I put up this night at one Pridie's, a sorry tavern; I had for company an idiot, the landlord's brother, who was himself but one remove from it, and I was waited on by an ugly broken backed old negro woman. My fare was indifferent, and as I was kept awake a great part of the night by bugs and fleas, and the united groaning and grunting of the hogs under the window, and my man Ben in the chamber with me; all this agreeable music was enlivened by perpetual peals of thunder and the rattling of heavy rain on the shingles over my head, which continued nearly the whole night, and began just as I entered the tavern.*

Undeterred by his night of horror, Smith continued on his journey the next day, crossing into North Carolina. His journal continues:

> *Ascending a very steep hill on the other side I entered the State of North Carolina. The road is there good. Stopt and breakfasted at Grant's store, twelve miles, where I got a very good breakfast and where a tavern is kept. About a mile further is a fork; the left goes on by Stublefield's tavern to Guilford Court House; the right, which I took, goes likewise to Guilford, by the iron works, and is reckoned a better road; it goes likewise to Salem.*

The ironworks Smith mentions was the Speedwell Furnace, often called the Troublesome Iron Works. Its remains are located in present-day Rockingham County near Monroeton. It was in operation as early as 1770 and supplied iron for the Revolutionary War effort. American general Nathanael Greene knew it well, having camped there twice in 1781 as he maneuvered the American forces under his command against those led by British general Charles Cornwallis. Because of its significance in the war effort, President George Washington visited it a few months after Smith did while on his southern tour.

According to his journal, Smith remained overnight at Troublesome Creek before resuming his journey the next day, Thursday, May 5. His trip would take him to Dobson's and then on to Salem. His comments about his ride through this vicinity provide interesting details about the landscape he observed as he approached the Cross Roads and the people he met along the way:

> *About two miles from the iron works the road again forks; the left leads to Guilford Court House, the right to Salem. Leaving the iron works, I ascended a high hill; the road for seventeen or eighteen miles towards Salem is very disagreeable—a soft clay badly cut up by the wagons, numberless stumps, some steep hills, the ascent obstructed by large stones. After passing a mill the road becomes very good, and continues so to Dobson's, about twenty-six miles from the iron works. There is no tavern in the whole of this distance, and the road a very long and fatiguing one, which took me six hours, so that I did not get my breakfast till after twelve. The country from Dix's ferry is well settled, many new plantations. The people, however, do not look so well as those more northerly, nor so much at their ease. The soil on the high land, indifferent, but good near the water courses. Country woody, now and then an opening, with a plantation of good-looking wheat, and sometimes from the summits of the hills, over which the road passes, is seen a great extent of woody country rising in waves one above the other, with a little clearing here and there.*

Finally, Smith arrived at the Cross Roads, where he recorded this: "I got a very good breakfast at Dobson's; he has a very decent house; his wife, who sat down to breakfast with me, is a huge fat woman of about eighty, whom he calls 'Honey.'"

Given that Smith was not the least bit shy about criticizing his accommodations, it seems clear that William and Martha Dobson served him a good meal and offered a touch of personal hospitality to boot. Thus, it would seem that their tavern was one of the better ones in that part of the country. Smith was wrong in his conjecture about Mrs. Dobson's age, although she could have appeared well advanced in years. It is known that her son, William Polk Dobson, was born in 1783. If Martha had indeed been eighty years old in 1791, she would have been seventy-two years old when her son was born, which is clearly impossible.

The most distinguished figure ever to sit down in Dobson's was George Washington. His visit was occasioned by his tour of southern states carried out in 1791. During the course of two previous tours, the president had visited New England and Long Island. Now, it was time for him to become acquainted with the southern states.

According to his diary, Washington wanted to visit the South "to acquire knowledge of the face of the country, the growth and agriculture thereof—and the temper and disposition of the inhabitants toward the new government." He also hoped it would help build support for the struggling new federal government.

Following the establishment of the new national government, one of the first tasks facing the president and the Congress was to find a way to support it and build confidence in its financial stability. Washington entrusted the task to his secretary of the treasury, Alexander Hamilton. Hamilton's plan was enacted into law when the first Congress adjourned in March 1791, but there was considerable trepidation over how the public would react to it. Hamilton and the other Federalists turned to Washington's tremendous popularity with the old soldiers and plain citizens to help them build a strong central government. Indeed, affection for Washington was one factor that convinced an undecided public in North Carolina to ratify the Constitution, and it was hoped that his southern tour would help win approval for Hamilton's plan.

Washington recorded the private record of his tour in his diary, but unlike Smith, he limited most entries to objective facts, even though he certainly had personal opinions about his observations. From his diary, it is learned that a thirty-one-mile journey on May 31, 1791, brought the president from Salisbury to the Moravian town of Salem, where his visit caused much excitement. According to Adelaide Fries, "Washington chose to include Salem on his tour because of the better conditions of the roads in that area and to show his friendliness towards the Moravians, whose sincere neutrality in the Revolution had distinguished them from the loyalist element." No doubt he was also appreciative of their efforts in supplying the American forces during that conflict.

The president and his party departed Salem on the morning of June 2. His destination was Guilford County, where he wanted to visit the site where the Battle of Guilford Courthouse was fought on March 15, 1781. His diary reads:

> *Thursday 2d. In company with the Govr. I set out by 4 Oclock for Guilford. Breakfasted at one Dobsons at the distance of eleven miles from Salem and dined at Guilford 16 miles farther, where there was a considerable gathering of people who had receivd notice of my intention to be there to day & came to satisfy their curiosity. On my way I examined the ground on which the Action between Generals Green and Lord Cornwallis commenced and after dinner rode over that where their lines were formed and the scene closed in the retreat of the American forces—The first line of which was advantageously drawn up, and had the Troops done their duty properly, the British must have been sorely galded in their advance, if not defeated.*

Washington, like Smith before him, also recorded his observations regarding the landscape through which he journeyed, including that around

Circa 1966 photo showing Dobson's Tavern following its removal in 1925 from its original site on the town square. *Courtesy of Mary Ruth Körner family.*

Cross Roads. Here, Washington states: "The Lands between Salem and Guilford are, in places, very fine; but upon the whole can not be called more than middling—some very bad." Washington also characterized the soil in the area as a "greasy red," a description of the clay in the vicinity that remains apt today.

The Cross Roads was an ideal site for an inn and tavern, and the one operated by Dobson was surely a hub of daily activity in that vicinity. While it provided the usual food, drink and shelter to travelers who called there, it would also have been a regular gathering place for local citizens, a place to greet friends and catch up on the latest news and gossip. Others visited the tavern seeking Dobson's services as an officer of the court, perhaps to have him witness an affidavit, will or deed. Some also came to have Dobson perform a marriage ceremony for them. In August 1858, Mary Whicker, widow of Revolutionary War soldier James Whicker, applied for a pension based on her husband's military service. In her affidavit in support of the application, she testified that "she intermarried with the said James Whicker in the month of June the 15th day in the year 1792 [and] the marriage was celebrated by William Dobson Esquire a Justice of the Peace in the County of Stokes NC." Mary added that she was born and brought up in that part of Stokes that is now Forsyth and had lived there her entire life and that her maiden name was Dean.

William Dobson and his wife continued to operate their tavern for another fifteen years after Washington's visit, until it was finally sold in 1806 to Gottlieb Schober, a Salem Moravian. During this time, the name Dobson continued to appear in the records. For example, the Salem board minutes of January 21, 1800, record that "Charles Bagge has informed the local directing boards that he is considering building near Michael Rominger, Jr. three miles from Salem on the big road to Dobsons, and would like to have the approval of our boards."

Following the sale to Schober, William and Martha Dobson moved back to their home plantation, where William died in 1822. His will, dated June 3, 1813, was proved in 1822 at the December term of Stokes County court. It directed that "my beloved wife Martha possess and enjoy the Plantation I now live on containing Two hundred Acres known by the name of Shepherd's hill, with all the profit and condiments Arising there from during her natural life—And at her death I give and bequeath the said plantation With all and singular appurtenances unto my son Henry Baker Dobson to him and his heirs forever." Witnesses were Archibald Campbell and Aaron Coffin, no doubt close friends and neighbors.

From local land records, it is known that Shepherd's Hill plantation was only a few miles northwest of Kernersville, making it very likely that it was in the vicinity of a road there today that bears the name Sheppard Hill. Perhaps more interesting is the fact that one of the most direct routes to the area where Sheppard Hill Road runs today is to take Dobson Street out of the town of Kernersville. In Dobson's day, this road was likely called Dobson's Road or, simply, the road to Dobson's.

William and Martha Dobson had two sons, Henry Baker and William Polk; the latter achieved the most public success. He was a lawyer, farmer and merchant of Rockford, in Surry County. He served in the North Carolina Senate between 1818 and 1842 and was a member of the state's constitutional convention in 1835. He married Mary Hughes and left many descendants, some of whom remain in the Kernersville area. An obituary for William Polk Dobson appeared in the March 21, 1846 *Greensboro Patriot*: "Died at his residence near Rockford, Surry County on the 1st day of March instant, William P. Dobson Esq., aged 63 on the 6th day of February last." He is buried in a family cemetery near Rockford.

Plunkett Place

The *Kernersville Bicentennial Book* offers the following account of the first school in the town:

> *About 1856, the Masons opened what is said to be the first school in Kernersville. It was a subscription school and parents supported it by paying a tuition. The School was at the old "Plunkett Place," which is now the site of the Pierce Funeral Home. The school was opened in a two-room house and one of the teachers during the period of operation was Miss Gaiselle Dicks from Randleman, North Carolina. Later she married Doctor Elias Kerner. She was the mother of the late Addie Kerner Adkins. Another teacher was Sarah Anne Mabry, the mother of the late J.M. Greenfield. According to reports this school continued throughout the Civil War period.*

Interestingly, this account is at variance with another found in *Joseph of Kernersville*:

> *Sometime between 1840 and 1848, John F. and Philip* [Kerner] *built a school house on* [the] *SW side of Mountain Road about 300 yards West of the Cross Roads. The construction was done by John Ross who lived in what is today known as the Edwards Place on the Oak Ridge road. In that building Wesley Ross, son of John Ross, taught school for several years,*

> *and many of the children of John F. and Philip attended. Among these were Philip's children, Gaston, Sally and Joseph J.*

Of these two, the second seems more plausible, as it is based on firsthand accounts—Joseph J. Körner, mentioned above, related this information directly to Jules Gilmer Körner, author of *Joseph of Kernersville*. According to the latter, in later years this site became known as the "Plunkett Place" and still later as the "Shore Place." It is worth noting the author's use of the term "site" in reference to the Plunkett home. This could mean the original schoolhouse was expanded to become the Plunkett Place or, more likely, that the Plunkett home was built on or near the property where this early school operated.

A map drawn by E.A. Vogler of Salem in 1863 shows what may be the original school location on present-day West Mountain Street, just west of the crossroads, and may be the building used as a school until the Kernersville High School opened in November 1858. As will be seen, some of the Plunkett property abutted other land referred to in various deeds as the "Public School Property," but it seems that was a later school that will be discussed in a subsequent story in this book.

It is known that by 1930, the old Shore home had become the Linville Funeral Home. Records show that, by 1910, Addison Newton Linville, or "Add" as he was locally known, was operating as an undertaker and embalmer in Kernersville. In 1911, this firm was operating as W.S. Linville & Son, but this business was located at that time on the north side of West Mountain Street, just west of its intersection with Main. In any case, by 1958 the old Plunkett home had become the Ragland Funeral Home, and today it is operated as the Pierce-Jefferson Funeral Home.

So what do the records say about the Plunkett family who lived in the house known as Plunkett Place? For one thing, they inform us that the owner's name was John F. Plunkett. Plunkett was born in Guilford County, North Carolina, in September 1834 and appears in the 1850 federal census there. Soon after, he moved to Winston in Forsyth County, where he went into the furniture and undertaking business. He did not remain there long before moving to Kernersville, where he was living in 1860, according to census records (he was listed as a "mechanic," age twenty-five years).

Plunkett appears in the Forsyth County land records on April 6, 1863, when he purchased more than three acres of land in Kernersville from

Plunkett Place as it appears today (2010) as part of the Pierce-Jefferson Funeral Home. *Photo by authors.*

William Campbell. The purchase price was $950. In the deed, the parcel was described as being taken "off of the land of Wm. P. Henly and adjoining the land of Joseph E. Kerner." This was part of the Cross Roads tract Henley had purchased from Philip Kerner in 1848 and was part of the property Philip had inherited from his father, Joseph. The land description in the deed to Plunkett refers to Kerner's line, as well as "a stone on the East side of a drain in the big Road." The "big Road" is probably what is now called West Mountain Street.

Plunkett may have purchased this property in anticipation of marriage, as the Forsyth County records show he married Sarah E. Boles a few months later on September 22, 1863. She is referred to as Miss Lizzie Boyles in a marriage notice in the *Western Democrat* that appeared October 20, 1863. This notice gives the date of marriage as September 24, 1863, so the earlier date is likely that of the marriage bond.

An undated picture of Plunkett Place shows it was a three-bay, two-story, frame house with exterior end chimneys.

An 1870 census lists John Plunkett, age thirty-five, living in Kernersville. In this record, his occupation is shown as cabinetmaker, which is another term for furniture maker. Also shown in his household is wife Sarah (age thirty), son Ernest (age four), daughter Flora (age two) and son Charley (age four months old).

Earliest known photo of Plunkett Place, probably taken during the 1870s. *Courtesy of Edgar Shore Jr.*

Plunkett was a citizen of some prominence, as the records show he was one of the town commissioners by 1872 and again in the years 1877–78. In 1878, he advertised his business as "Jno. F. Plunkett, cabinet work and undertaker." It was not uncommon for cabinetmakers to also make coffins and act as undertakers. Assuming he carried on the undertaking business at his residence, as seems likely, this would mark the first use of the Plunkett Place for that purpose. The 1880 census calls Plunkett a "furniture dealer," age forty-five years.

An 1886 *News & Farm* advertisement refers to him as "J.F. Plunkett, undertaker and furniture dealer, corner Mountain and Cherry," which confirms that he was operating from his home. He also continued his involvement in civic affairs, as he is listed as a trustee of the Kernersville Academy (formerly High School) in 1888. A newspaper advertisement in that same year for the Kernersville millinery firm of Griffith & Totten (Mrs. L.E. Griffith and Miss Belle Totten) notes that "when in need of our services we can be found at the residence of L.E. Griffith, Corner Mountain and Cherry Streets, Opposite J.F. Plunkett's furniture rooms." Plunkett was still living in Kernersville in 1890, when he advertised his cabinet works again.

However, soon after, he retired from business and moved to Richmond, Virginia, to live with his children.

The Forsyth County land records contain a deed made January 1, 1894, from J.F. Plunkett and his wife, Sarah E. Plunkett, of Virginia to H.E. Shore for two lots in Kernersville totaling more than two acres. The deed mentions R.E. Fentress's corner and line, the sidewalk on Cherry Street, the public school line and G.F. Kerner's line. Also conveyed in the same deed was a second parcel. Its description mentions the "Public School Property," G.F. Kerner's line and the "middle of Mountain road." R.E. Fentress is the Remus E. Fentress to whom Plunkett deeded two parcels of land in 1875, probably part of his three-plus-acre tract.

So what was this public school mentioned in these deeds? According to an account found in the *Kernersville Bicentennial Book*, a public or free school was opened in Kernersville in October 1892, and it stood adjacent to property that is today occupied by the Pierce-Jefferson Funeral Home. This school stood until 1906, when it burned, a story told elsewhere in this book.

The land records show that H.E. Shore executed a mortgage deed to Plunkett on February 9, 1894, and its satisfaction is recorded in the Forsyth County land records:

> *State of Virginia, City of Richmond: We, the widow and heirs-at-law of John F. Plunkett, deceased, do hereby declare that the mortgage deed executed to the said John F. Plunkett by H.E. Shore and wife, as recorded in your office in book 21, of mortgages, page 425, has been paid off and satisfied in full, and we do hereby authorize you to cancel the same upon the records of your office.*

This mortgage release is dated October 17, 1910, and is signed by Sarah E. Plunkett, E.L. Plunkett, Mrs. Flora Plunkett Garren and Wm. M. Plunkett.

So Henry E. Shore and his wife purchased the Plunkett property in 1894. Shore's wife was Nancy Ella Kerner, daughter of Dr. Elias Kerner and his wife, Parthia Gazelle Dicks. Henry Shore died November 14, 1919.

An old photo of the Henry Shore home reveals that the Plunkett house had been modified by the addition of Victorian features, including a corner tower on the left front of the house and a wraparound porch on the lower level.

Notice of the passing of John F. Plunkett appears in an obituary in the April 24, 1907 *Times Dispatch* of Richmond, Virginia:

Plunkett Place, circa 1890, following structural remodeling by owner Henry E. Shore. *Courtesy of Edgar Shore Jr.*

> *Mr. John F. Plunkett died at the residence of his son, Mr. W.M. Plunkett No. 412 North Twelfth Street, last night at 7 o'clock.*
>
> *He was born in Guilford County, N.C., in 1834, and was seventy-two years old.*
>
> *After reaching manhood, Mr. Plunkett went into the furniture and undertaking business at Winston, N.C., and later moved to Kernersville, N.C., where he lived until December, 1890, when he retired from business and came to Richmond to spend the remainder of his life with his children.*
>
> *Mr. Plunkett was a prominent Mason and Knight Templar, but since 1898, when he was stricken with paralysis, he was not able to attend to either. He is survived by his widow, one daughter and two sons—Messrs. W.M. and E.C. Plunkett, who are connected with the railway mail service here.*
>
> *The funeral arrangements have not yet been completed, but will be announced today. The funeral will take place tomorrow or Friday.*

Additional information about Plunkett appeared in the April 26 and 27, 1907 editions of the *Times Dispatch*. They record that he served during the Civil War in the Home Guards of Kernersville. John F. Plunkett was finally laid to rest in Hollywood Cemetery in Richmond.

A Man Who Could Heal Both Body and Soul

In Kernersville's earlier days, it was not unusual to find men who practiced more than one occupation simultaneously. A good example is Benjamin Jackson Sapp, who practiced medicine and also operated a drugstore and hotel in town.

Levi Isaac Bodenhamer was another such man. He was a descendant of Christian Bodenhamer, who was born in Germany about 1725. After immigrating to this country, Christian and his wife, Charity Beamer, settled in that part of Rowan County, North Carolina, that later became Davidson County. He and his wife are buried there in the cemetery at Abbotts Creek Primitive Baptist Church founded in 1756.

Levi was born April 6, 1831, the son of Levi and Emily Orrell Bodenhamer. When he reached manhood, he married Nancy F. Beeson, daughter of Hugh and Jane Beeson.

According to Robbins's 1888 sketch, Levi came to Kernersville about 1874. He had been a preacher in the Primitive Baptist Church for thirty-five years and was the first pastor of Saints Delight Church, serving from 1876 until 1889. He is mentioned in this capacity in an article written by the editor of the *Kernersville News* in June 1883:

> *On* [the] *1st Sunday morning, our kind and much esteemed young friend, Geo. Ray put his fine horse and new buggy at our disposal, and off we went to a baptizing in the neighborhood of a Primitive Baptist Church,*

Elder Levi Isaac Bodenhamer, first pastor of Saints Delight Primitive Baptist Church. He served until 1889. *Courtesy of Terry Motsinger.*

known as Saints Delight. After the immersion, we followed the train of a large concourse of people and soon found ourselves at the church which was some half mile distant. The church is situated in the forks of two country roads, on a beautiful elevation and surrounded by a lovely forest. It was built about 10 years ago and will do credit to any country church, but it is entirely too small for those who assemble there on preaching occasions. Not more than half of the congregation could be seated last Sunday and we are informed that such is frequently the case. Elder L.I. Bodenhamer of this place preached a very able sermon; forcible and full of sound logical reasoning. It was most assuredly a very great pleasure to us to attend the services, such good order prevailed, not a particle of disturbance but all seemed to realize the fact that they were in the house of the Lord in his

The second Saints Delight Church, completed in 1905. It served the congregation until 1952, when it was replaced by the present brick church building. *Courtesy of Terry Motsinger.*

> *immediate presence. After the services, we met with N.B. Orrell Esq. of Abbotts Creek, Davidson Co. We had dinner with him and after taking refreshments, the large crowd dispersed home.*

N.B. Orrell mentioned above was Napoleon Bonaparte Orrell, whose wife was Christina L. Motsinger. He was a stepbrother to Levi Bodenhamer's wife Emily.

Not content with healing only the soul, Bodenhamer also carried on a medical practice in Kernersville, which he began about 1863. During the winter of 1887–88, he traveled to Baltimore, Maryland, where he attended a course of lectures at the College of Physicians and Surgeons. If the description contained in an old newspaper card of June 1888 is any indication, the lectures were comprehensive for that time and place:

> *Dr. L.I. Bodenhamer announces to the citizens of Kernersville and surrounding country that he is now better prepared for the practice of medicine than he has been for the past twenty-five years having attended a full course of medical lectures in the "College of Physicians and Surgeons" in Baltimore, Md., the past fall and winter and being a resident student*

> *and boarder in the "City Hospital" in Baltimore, where he had full access to all the works of the institution. And having taken a full special private course on "Physical Diagnoses," under Prof. John S. Lynch, M.D., together with studies, and lectures upon the following subjects to wit:—Surgery, Anatomy and Genito Urinary Surgery, Practice of Medicine and Clinical Affections* [sic] *of the Chest and Throat, Physiology and Diseases of Children, Diseases of Eye and Ear, Obstetrics and Diseases of Women, Clinical Medicine and Diseases of Nervous System, Materia Medica, Theraputics* [sic] *and Mental Diseases, Chemistry and Toxicology, Hygiene, Dermatology, Medical Jurisprudence, and Pathology. Also having purchased a good library on medicines and diseases written by the most thorough, scientific and practical authors—both American and European. He therefore feels better prepared to serve the public in the general practice of medicine, than he has in the past twenty-five years. He is now located in Kernersville, on Main Street, west of the Moravian Church. All calls promptly responded to either day or night. Charges reasonable and service faithful. In all cases, where the interest of the patient requires it consultation with other physicians of professional character, will be called for.*

Dr. Bodenhamer was also an inventor and is the recognized owner of at least nine United States patents: Improvement in Washing-Machines (No. 122,431, January 2, 1872); Reciprocating Churn (No. 140,880, July 15, 1873); Bale Tie and Hoop-Lacer (No. 170,932, December 14, 1875); Stalk Trimmer and Cutter (No. 205,470, July 2, 1878); Plow (No. 277,205, May 8, 1883); Car Coupling (No. 279,217, June 12, 1883); Compound for Preserving Eggs (No. 326,895, September 22, 1885); Medicine Case (No. 444,216, January 6, 1891); and Fertilizer Distributer [*sic*] and Grain Drill (No. 500,557, July 4, 1893).

In the description of his "Compound for Preserving Eggs," it is revealed that "the compound or solution in question is composed of water, lime, salt, saltpeter, decoction of oak-bark, and powered charcoal, into which the eggs are to be placed and kept until desired for use." Whether this formula was effective or even used is unknown.

His patent called "Medicine Case" was for a portable medicine cabinet that was designed "to provide a neat, simple, and inexpensive cabinet for the use of physicians in visiting the sick, whereby any number of bottles containing tinctures and other medicines may be carried."

As noted earlier, Dr. B.J. Sapp was at one time the owner of a hotel. This establishment was operated in what was left of William Dobson's original 1788 tavern at the Cross Roads. A sketch of Kernersville published in the *Winston-Salem Journal* in 1920 reveals that Dr. Bodenhamer was also one of the several owners of this tavern, acquiring it from Jule Gray. The latter bought it from William P. Henley, who acquired it in 1848 from Philip Kerner.

After a full and productive life, Dr. Levi Isaac Bodenhamer passed away on September 17, 1900. His children included daughters Emma, Flora, Lucetta, Cornelia E. and Nannie E. and sons Ogden Levi James Madison, William M. and Julius Gray. Fittingly, he is buried in Saints Delight Primitive Baptist Church Cemetery near Kernersville.

Dunlap's Mineral Springs

Some Kernersville old-timers still recall youthful visits to a local mineral springs and the resort that grew up around it in the early 1920s. Known as Dunlap's Mineral Springs, the complex sported a two-story brick hotel with a ballroom and dining facility, as well as a swimming pool.

The story of the Dunlap family, from whom the springs take their name, begins with a gentleman named Samuel Dunlap, who moved from Moore to Chatham County, North Carolina, sometime prior to 1830. He had two grandsons: John H. Dunlap (December 22, 1858–January 4, 1930) and Isaac Hunter Dunlap (1865–1946), called "Ike." Both settled in the area of Chatham County now called Bonlee, where they bought 2,545 acres of first-growth timber and built homes, a sawmill, a planer and a cotton gin. The vicinity was first called Dunlap Mills but was later changed to Causey in honor of an early resident.

Ike Dunlap built a flour, meal and feed mill along the tracks of the Cape Fear and Yadkin Valley Railroad and made Causey a stop. But disliking the name Causey, Ike offered a barrel of his best "White Daisy Flour" as a prize to anyone coming up with something better. Finally, a shoe salesman named Glazebrook suggested Bonlee—"Bon" meaning good and "Lee" meaning breeze. The town was incorporated in 1930, and Ike served as its first mayor.

The two Dunlap brothers continued to make money from their timber business and eventually owned a twelve-square-mile area. However, they needed something more efficient than mule teams to get their timber to

Circa 1925 postcard view of the Dunlap Springs Hotel. *Courtesy of Wayne Biby.*

Circa 1925 postcard view of the lobby of the Dunlap Springs Hotel. *Courtesy of Wayne Biby.*

Circa 1925 postcard view of the dining room of the Dunlap Springs Hotel. *Courtesy of Wayne Biby.*

market, so they decided to build their own railroad—the Bonlee and Western Railroad—which opened in 1910. It operated until the mid-1930s, when a combination of factors—the Depression, hard-surfaced roads and increased truck traffic—forced it out of business.

Looking to extend his business enterprise beyond the bounds of Chatham County, John H. Dunlap purchased two parcels of land near Kernersville. The first was a seventy-three-acre tract bought in 1914, while the second consisted of sixty-four acres purchased in 1915. The mineral springs were located on the latter, and that is where the other facilities associated with the resort were located.

The exact date when construction of the hotel began is unknown, but a story that appeared in the May 23, 1920 edition of the *Winston-Salem Journal* indicates that work was underway by that date. According to the story:

> [Kernersville] *has other attractions to offer people after the day's work is done, however, for within a mile of the town is Dunlap Springs, which gives promise of becoming one of the most popular resorts in the Piedmont Section. A new fire-proof hotel is being erected on the high hill that overlooks the spring. Nearby will be a spacious dance-hall, which should become a fashionable rendezvous for the people of High Point, Greensboro, Winston-Salem and other nearby cities. Then, too, there are three important cities within a fifteen mile radius, and these are easily accessible. It is believed*

Dunlap's mineral springs. People believed its waters were good for the health. Kernersville Bicentennial Book *photo, 1971.*

> *that the summer guests of Dunlap Springs will become great boosters of Kernersville after the vacation season ends and they return to their homes.*

A 1924 alumni history of the University of North Carolina lists Henry Hunter Dunlap (September 15, 1899–June 25, 1964), son of Ike Dunlap and his wife, Cora Flack, as the hotel's bookkeeper.

The resort remained a popular destination for tourists throughout most of the 1920s and was still in full swing in April 1926, when H.J. Goldston and J.W. Goldston Jr. filed a partnership agreement in the Forsyth County deed office to operate the Dunlap Springs Hotel.

However, like countless other businesses, the popular resort fell on hard times when the Great Depression struck in 1929, and the hotel was closed. According to Forsyth County land records, John H. Dunlap and his wife, Mary Lea Dunlap, mortgaged the sixty-four acres in June 1927 but later defaulted on the payment of the indebtedness, and the property was sold at a public sale on October 20, 1931.

The hotel remained closed until 1934, when it was pressed into use by the North Carolina Emergency Relief Administration (ERA) to house jobless men. A history of the ERA written in 1936 provides this bit of information:

The Carolina Serenaders, one of the many dance bands that entertained guests at the Dunlap Springs Hotel during the Roaring Twenties. *Courtesy of Gloria Lowrey.*

> *As the fall of 1934 approached, the number of men in the transient centers increased rapidly, and the camp facilities were inadequate to take care of the load; therefore it became increasingly necessary that some way be found to occupy the leisure time of these men, in order to keep them off the streets, and thus allay community criticism. In September a State Recreation Director was employed who worked throughout the state getting new programs started and simulating those already in existence.*
>
> *To take care of the overflow in Greensboro, the buildings of a closed summer hotel at Dunlap Springs, about fifteen miles from Greensboro, were rented to provide needed quarters. Old and infirm men were sent there. The men who were able to work repaired and reconditioned the buildings, cleaned up the grounds, consisting of 60 acres, planted shrubbery and trimmed trees. The spring at this camp has proved a great help to these older men. Their general health has improved and at this time there has been no illness of* [a] *serious nature.*

Elsewhere, the history notes that Thurman P. Warren was the director of the Dunlap Springs ERA facility. Known locally as T.P. Warren, he later settled in Kernersville, where he operated an automobile dealership.

In September 1935, the government began to close its transient centers and return men to their homes. Employable persons were certified for work on Works Progress Administration projects. By February 1, 1936, all centers were closed except Dunlap Springs. It remained open until the end of March of that year, when it, too, was closed.

The property passed through several hands, but by December 30, 1940, it belonged to Mrs. A.D. Gallimore and her husband, L.B. Gallimore, both of Guilford County. On that date, the Gallimores deeded the sixty-four-acre tract and its buildings to the trustees of the Southern District of the Pilgrim Holiness Church. The description in the deed called it "the Dunlap Mineral Springs property." The property was purchased for use as a church college and high school. About this same time, the seventy-three-acre tract purchased by John H. Dunlap in 1914 was subdivided into building lots known as the Dunlap Springs Development and sold off to individual purchasers.

The buildings conveyed to the Pilgrim Holiness trustees in 1941 were in need of significant repair before they could be used, and it was not until

Circa 1955 postcard view of the Dunlap Springs Hotel building following its conversion to use as the Southern Pilgrim Bible College. *Courtesy of Wayne Biby.*

1946 that the college opened its doors. An article in the September 12, 1946 edition of the *Landmark*, a Statesville, North Carolina newspaper, mentions the event:

> *Mr. and Mrs. C.E. Vernon and sons, Carlis and Kennard, and Mr. and Mrs. James Shoaltz were in Kernersville Tuesday evening to attend a convocation at Pilgrim Bible College at Dunlap Springs near Kernersville. This property, recently acquired by the Pilgrim church, is the new Pilgrim Bible College, offering college and high school courses and special courses in Bible. Leroy Vernon, son of Mr. and Mrs. Vernon, is a student in the high school department.*

For the next twenty-five years, both a high school and Bible college were operated at Dunlap Springs, during which time several other buildings were added to the complex. In 1956, the school's name was changed to Southern Pilgrim Bible College and then to Kernersville Wesleyan College in 1970.

In 1968, the Pilgrim Holiness Church and the Wesleyan Methodist Church united to form the Wesleyan Church. As a result, further changes were made to educational institutions operated by the two churches that merged. It was decided that the college at Kernersville would be closed, and it ceased operation in 1971, when it was merged into United Wesleyan College in Allentown, Pennsylvania. The high school continued in operation on the same campus under the name Kernersville Wesleyan Academy until 1981, when it merged into the Wesleyan Education Center (Wesleyan Christian Academy) in High Point.

In 1984, the campus was sold to Dudley Cosmetology University, part of a larger business enterprise operated by Dudley Products, a hair care and cosmetics business founded and operated by black entrepreneurs Joe L. Dudley and his wife, Eunice Mosley Dudley. The Grady P. Swisher Center of Forsyth Technical Community College is also located at the site today.

As for the actual springs themselves, they were covered over during the construction of I-40 and the exit from it onto Highway 421 toward Greensboro, according to longtime Kernersville resident Moir Whicker. At the time, the springs were capped and the water piped up to the college. Eventually, the water supply dwindled and was replaced with Kernersville city water.

Elias Kerner Huff

A Man of Many Talents

"A musical carpenter with an artistic bent" is how an article in the May 24, 1942 *Winston-Salem Journal* described Elias Kerner Huff of Kernersville. Indeed, he was not only a highly skilled woodworker, a talented painter and a gifted musician with his own band, but he was also the inventor of what might be described as a forerunner of the modern automobile-drawn trailer or camper that served both as an art studio and an on-the-road residence. Some claim Huff was named after an early Kernersville physician, Dr. Elias Kerner, which seems likely even though there is no evident connection between the two family lines.

Born in Forsyth County, North Carolina, on November 16, 1856, Elias was the son of David and Matilda (Smith) Huff. He appears in the 1860 census for the Northern Division of Davidson County in the household of his father, who is listed there as "D.M. Huff," age twenty-six.

Elias was but a boy of nine years when his father died, leaving him to help his widowed mother support his younger siblings, a sister Martha and brother Hickson. In fact, David Huff died on March 16, 1865, shot by a Confederate firing squad only a few weeks before the end of the Civil War. Little is known of the circumstances surrounding his death. The graveyard register of Friedland Moravian Church, where Huff is buried, notes that he was shot by members of the First North Carolina Sharpshooters Battalion, and the inscription on his stone there confirms it: "David Huff, Born April 5th 1833, Killed by the Rebels, March 16th, 1865." Newspaper accounts of the day report that the Sharpshooters, under the command of Captain Reuben E. Wilson, had been in the vicinity rounding up deserters, but David Huff was a civilian. R.P. Leinbach, minister of Friedland when the shooting occurred, noted in his diary on March 18, 1865, that "our community was shocked on hearing that David Huff and 4 other men had been shot by order of Capt. Wilson. I was sorely distressed for poor David Huff and his deeply afflicted family, as I believed him to have been innocent of the charge of instigating the expedition for the release of J. Huff, a deserter." No definitive evidence has emerged that would identify "J. Huff," although there is some suggestion he may have been David's brother, Jordan Huff.

For all families living in the South after the war, times were hard, and especially so for a widow with young children. By 1870, Matilda was living with Elias and her two other children in Abbotts Creek Township of Forsyth County, where Elias was a farmhand. While he had few opportunities for formal education, he took advantage of those presented to him to hone his natural gifts for music and art, which in later life provided his livelihood.

Elias's mother, Matilda, married again on September 2, 1875, this time to Alfred L. Swaim. Not long after, on February 6, 1876, Elias married a young

The Israel Kerner Hotel, where Elias Kerner Huff and wife lived before construction of their home on South Main Street. The hotel burned in 1912. *Courtesy of Gloria Lowrey.*

The Elias Kerner Huff house in its original location on South Main Street before its removal to its present Pineview Street location. *Courtesy of Ellen Cook.*

lady from Union Cross named Clementine Sells, called "Clem" by family and friends. Following their marriage, the couple moved to Kernersville, where they occupied a room at the old Israel Kerner Hotel at the "Y" in Kernersville (this is where present-day South Main and Salisbury Streets meet). They lived there until they moved into their first home on South Main. It had two rooms, but others were added over the years.

The 1880 Kernersville census shows that Elias was working as a coach painter. His employer was Anderson Lewis, who operated a carriage-making enterprise there. According to *Joseph of Kernersville*, Anderson Lewis and William A. Griffith became partners in coachmaking in Kernersville and, about 1857, built their plant and homes on Salisbury Street.

Huff must have impressed his employer, because by 1885 they were in business together. According to the *People's Press* of February 19, 1885:

> *Mr. Anderson Lewis and Elias Huff have gone into co-partnership in the buggy business, and in addition they have incorporated Mr. Harrell's*

> *wagon establishment, and I saw the first installment in the way of wagons standing at this shop the other day, they are first class, and no mistake, if any one wants a good wagon, and a neatly finished up job, there is the place to get it—they mean business.*

It seems the firm quickly made a name for itself, as another piece in the *People's Press* on July 23, 1885, illustrates: "Lewis & Huff have just re-painted and sent home an Omnibus for the Central Hotel at Winston, and have another one on hand for the same place. Their work is getting a reputation in a great portion of this State and Virginia, and Mr. Huff ranks as a first class painter. The one sent out speaks for itself and the other will when he is done with it." Also interesting is that while Huff and Anderson were in business together, they entered a patent in the United States Patent Office for what they called "certain new and useful Improvements in Buggies." Application for this patent (No. 328321) was filed on August 31, 1885, and issued October 13, 1885.

It is not clear why, but the partnership between Lewis and Huff was dissolved after a year or two, at which time Huff went into business with John Robert L. Stuart of Kernersville. Stuart, born in Guilford County on October 11, 1862, and called "Bob" by his acquaintances, was a blacksmith and ironworker by trade. According to a memoir of his life:

> *He lived with his widowed mother at their Deep River, Guilford County home until he was 16 years of age, when he came here to Kernersville, seeking employment. He learned the trade of mechanic, at which he worked successfully for many years. For a time he was in East Bend, N.C., then with the White Vehicle Company of Winston-Salem. He and the late Elias Huff made buggies and wagons in Kernersville, the former being a painter, especially of vehicles. For a time also our brother was in the employ of the S.J. Nissen Wagon Company of Winston-Salem.*

Bob Stuart married Ora Belle Hendrix, and they lived in a two-story frame house on the north side of Bodenhamer Street that was torn down in the 1950s. The Stuarts had several children, including Ned, who for many years was the Kernersville fire chief, and Elizabeth, who married Basil Hedgecock of High Point and later taught school in Kernersville.

The *News & Farm* of Kernersville ran an interesting story about the partnership between Huff and Stuart in its October 7, 1887 edition under the heading "Huff and Stuart's Buggy Works":

> *One of the most enterprising, pushing firms in town is that of Huff and Stuart, manufacturers of buggies, phaetons, road-carts, &c. E.K. Huff and J.R. Stuart, although young men have had several years of experience and are practical workmen, acquainted with every detail of their business.*
>
> *Last spring they erected, near the depot, in full view of the railroad, one of the most conveniently arranged buildings for their business that could have been conceived. It is a large building, well lighted, well ventilated and possessing attractiveness and convenience in a marked degree. The office, work-shop, room for dry lumber and large division for finished work, occupy the first floor. An elevator, designed and built throughout by the firm, carries work to and from the second floor. On this floor, we find the trimming room, furnished with a new Singer machine, the paint and finishing room, drying room and large hall for finished work, the end of which a large door on pulleys opens out upon a well-braced porch. The smith-shop, in which Mr. Stuart spends his whole time, is near by, fitted out with the most improved appliances for that kind of work. He is said to be one of the finest mechanics in the State. Few can iron a buggy any more quickly or neatly.*
>
> *Mr. Huff has a reputation far and near as an artistic painter. He has painted several omnibuses for Winston and Greensboro hotel men and has never failed to give satisfaction as well as excite admiration. He is a genius and is always adding to his stack of information. Even now he is pursuing the study of art and landscape painting under one specially qualified to teach it. As the designer of the Trotting-Buggy, he has constructed a cheap, durable buggy, not excelled, for the price, anywhere.*
>
> *As we said before, Huff & Stuart are young men. They have gone to considerable expense to get fixed for business. They are honest, hard-working young men, who do honest, homemade work and do it cheap. They are entitled to the patronage of the public, because they will appreciate it and will make a good return for it. We want to see them succeed, because they deserve it and because it is an enterprise founded on muscle and honest endeavor. Give them a lift!*

The 1887 Huff and Stuart carriage works building on Bodenhamer Street. This photo, taken circa 1923, also shows Kernersville's fire company testing its new equipment. *Courtesy of Robert U. Stuart.*

The building erected by Huff and Stuart was located on Bodenhamer Street immediately north of the Reid and Harmon roller mill. This two-story frame building was later used by W.F. "Billy" Winfree, who lived next door to it, and R. Shepherd "Shep" Nelson as a broom factory.

Robbins's 1888 sketch included the following description of Huff and Stuart's carriage manufacturing operation:

> *E.K. Huff is a native of this country, and has had over a dozen years of experience as a carriage upholsterer, trimmer and painter. He was for five years a partner with Mr. Lewis, as Lewis & Huff, and a year since, in company with J.R. Stuart of Forsyth county he opened up trade south of the depot. The firm erected a neat two story building, equipped with elevator and modern requisites, where they are prepared to turn out all kinds of custom work in the most approved manner. Mr. Stuart has had nine years experience as a blacksmith and*

superintends that department which is conducted in a detached building near the factory. Many of his well-wrought hammers and other tools are of his own manufacture evincing genius at the forge. The new firm are prepared to do good work and will spare no effort to meet the requirements of the trade.

It is not known just how long Elias Huff and Bob Stuart remained in business together, but eventually both went their separate ways. Stuart later operated a blacksmith shop and ironworks on Bodenhamer Street until about a year before his death on February 26, 1939.

Elias Huff went to Winston-Salem, where he joined the S.J. Nissen Wagon Company and worked there as the company's draftsman and artist. He also did upholstering work and executed the lettering on the ice and delivery wagons manufactured by Nissen. Wagon making had been a prominent industrial activity in the Waughtown community of Winston-Salem since the 1830s, when three wagon works were located there, including one operated by the Nissen family. John Phillip Nissen began wagon production in 1834, and five of his sons followed him in that trade. His youngest, Samuel Jacob Nissen, first went into the tobacco business, but in October 1890, he purchased property at the corner of East Third Street and Depot Street (now Patterson Avenue). There, in 1895, he completed a three-story brick building, with two basements, and used it as a wagon-making and repair shop and carriage repository until the late 1920s, when the truck overtook the wagon as a means of commercial conveyance.

Elias Kerner Huff's mobile studio, often called his "house on wheels." It was built in 1906. *Courtesy of Ellen Cook.*

Another view of Huff's mobile studio.
Courtesy of Ellen Cook.

Just when Huff went to work for Nissen is not known, but it was sometime before January 9, 1906, when a short item appeared in the *Winston-Salem Journal* that described his novel, horse-drawn house on wheels mentioned earlier:

> *Mr. E.K. Huff the draftsman and artist for Nissen and Roan, this city, builders of the fanciest and best wagons built in the South, has determined to begin living out doors, and to this end is having built a studio on wheels. He drew the design himself and it will be finished in about 30 days.*
>
> *It will be 6½ by 16 feet and fitted up as a living room and office. He will locate first on A.C. Green's lot No. 216 Elm street, moving as his fancy dictates. All of his designing will be done in this novel studio, which is to be beautiful in design and workmanship.*

Henry Roan, who had been an early partner of R.J. Reynolds in the tobacco business, was also a partner in S.J. Nissen's venture during the years 1902–6, according to various Winston-Salem city directories.

Other stories about Huff appeared in the May 24, 1942 issue of the *Winston-Salem Journal* and in the *People's News* of Kernersville, which carried this story:

> [Huff's] *trailer home was moved from place to place by horses. When Mr. Huff returned to Kernersville to resume his work in his carriage shop—which was later a garage when automobiles had appeared on the streets—the studio was brought to the city with the aid of four horses driven by Bob Taylor (colored). Passengers on this eventful trip were: Mrs. J.C. Ragland, Miss. Joyce Huff now Mrs. Everett Coren of Concord, North Carolina Phin, Charlie James, Bayne Ragland and John Huff.*
>
> *After being used on his home site for several years Mr. Huff sold the studio to Mr. Hester, a traveling salesman. The studio was always a place of interest to passerbys.*

As noted earlier, Elias and Clem built their house in Kernersville on South Main Street. It originally stood where the visitors' center for the new Paul J. Ciener Botanical Gardens is being built today (2010) but was moved to a site on Pineview Street in Kernersville, where it has been restored. Gwynne Taylor, author of the 1981 book *From Frontier to Factory: An Architectural History of Forsyth County*, called the Elias Kerner Huff house "perhaps the best extant Victorian cottage in the county." There was a workshop at the rear of the house where Elias did many kinds of work, especially upholstering, and it is said he designed and built some of the furniture for the eclectic house called Körner's Folly that stood nearby.

Elias Kerner Huff was not only a talented artist but a skilled musician as well. He used this ability to organize and conduct two different bands during his lifetime. They made many appearances around the state, at times playing music at Moravian Easter sunrise services. The bands held weekly practices in a small room adjacent to his residence, known as the "Band Room." In later years, the room was incorporated into the dwelling itself.

After a long and productive life, Elias Kerner Huff passed away on February 7, 1920. He and his wife had two children, a son named Charles Lyndon Huff and a daughter, Manerva. Clementine Huff lived for another sixteen years following the death of her husband. She died on November 7, 1936. Both Elias and his wife are buried in Kernersville at Mount Gur Cemetery.

Hooker Furniture Complex

The complex of brick buildings on North Main Street in Kernersville, referred to today as the Hooker Furniture Complex, or "the Factory," has a history stretching back to the last quarter of the nineteenth century. The book *Joseph of Kernersville* offers this description of how the oldest building in the complex came into being:

> [In 1873] *W.H. Leak of Guilford erected a brick factory for the manufacture of tobacco. In 1880 he was joined by B. Alonzo Brown and N.W. Sapp as partners under the firm name of W.H. Leak & Co. In 1882 J.N. Leak (a brother) purchased the interest of N.W. Sapp and in 1884 the Leak brothers purchased B.A. Brown's interest. The factory was on the East side of Danville Street (now North Main Street).*

This statement suggests that the oldest building in the complex was erected in 1873. If so, then there is some question about the building referred to in a subsequent section of Körner's book: "[In 1884] B.A. Brown and N.W. Sapp, who had sold their interests in W.H. Leak & Co. (in 1882 and 1884) joined in partnership with J. Van Lindley of Pomona and built a large factory on [the] East side of Danville Street and engaged in the manufacture of tobacco under the firm name of Brown, Sapp & Co."

Fortunately, there is another mention of the Leak tobacco factory in a narration by George P. Winfree of Kernersville in the December 21, 1959 edition of the *People's News*. The editor of this paper was P.J. "Pete" Nash, a Leak family descendant who lived in the old Leak home on South Main Street. This house once stood on the southeast corner of Harmon Lane and South Main Street. In describing Kernersville in former days, Winfree commented: "Where the Leak home (Pete Nash's home) stood there was a tobacco factory on the back part of the lot. The Leak Tobacco Factory was the first in this area even before R.J. Reynolds Tobacco Factory. This building had a tower and was an octagon shaped building. The Leak home was just as it is today at its present location, only a tobacco factory on the back part of the lot."

The Leak house on South Main Street in a photo taken in 1944. Kernersville's first tobacco factory stood behind the house. Kernersville Bicentennial Book *photo, 1971.*

Based on Winfree's statement, it appears the tobacco factory that stood behind the old Leak home was the one erected in 1873 and that it was not until 1884 that the first building in the present Hooker Furniture building complex was erected on North Main Street.

Robbins's 1888 sketch of Kernersville seems to confirm this. Among the descriptions included there is one of W.H. Leak & Co. and another of Brown, Sapp & Co. Körner himself probably relied, at least in part, on the descriptions compiled by Robbins, which read as follows:

> *W.H. Leak & Co.*
> *Plug and Twist Tobacco*
>
> *W.H. and J.N. Leak are natives of Guilford county, the former having been engaged in the manufacture of tobacco in Stokes county for several years prior to opening the first factory here, in 1873. The enterprise was run by W.H. Leak until 1880, when B.A. Brown and N.W. Sapp were accepted as partners under firm style of W.H, Leak & Co. J.N. Leak was an assistant in the early part of the business here but subsequently was in merchandising at Lexington for 5 years and returning here in 1882 he purchased N.W. Sapp's interest in the factory. Two years later the Leak Brothers bought out Mr. Brown's interest continuing the old firm style of W.H. Leak & Co. Employment is given to 50 or 60 hands and the annual output is about 100,000 pounds of fine grade tobacco which is sold to wholesale jobbers. W.H. Leak has charge of the leaf purchases and his long experience has made him an expert in that line. J.N. looks after office matters and all departments of the trade are under careful supervision. A leading specialty in brands is "Leak's Best," 12 inch 3's and "Cock of the Walk," (Broad Gauge) 10 inch 4's.*
>
> *BROWN, SAPP & Co.*
> *Tobacco Manufacturers*
>
> *As mentioned under a former notice B.A. Brown and N.W. Sapp were formerly in the tobacco manufacture in company with W.H. Leak. Having retired from that firm they in 1884 in company with J. Van Lindley, of the Pomona nurseries, near Greensboro, built the large brick factory near the depot and opened up manufacture in that line. The structure is 40 x 90*

> *three stories in height and with rear addition of 40 x 16 feet. The firm works 50–60 hands turning out about 100,000 pounds annually. Among their standard brands are "Good News," "Jenny Lind," "Tube Rose," "Knights of Labor" and others. Institutions of this kind are important factors in the prosperity of the place.*

Robbins states that W.H. Leak & Co. opened its first factory in 1873 but does not say it was erected on North Main Street, as Körner seems to suggest. Moreover, Robbins states that Brown, Sapp & Co. built its factory near the depot, and this is likely the building still standing on North Main Street.

Yet another description of W.H. Leak & Co. can be found in the *Kernersville Bicentennial Book*, and it further confirms that the present building was put up in 1884:

> *W.H. Leak & Co.*
> *Plug and Twist Tobacco*
>
> *W.H. (Mr. Bill) Leak was the guiding spirit of this firm and associated with him at various times were J.N. Leak, B.A. Brown and N.W. Sapp. This business started in Kernersville in 1873. It appears that Brown, Sapp & Co. built the three story building on Main Street in 1884. This was later the W.H. Leak factory and more recently it was converted by Mr. Leak to a knitting mill. W.H. Leak & Co. tobacco brands were Leak's Best and Cock of the Walk. Their building is now used in the operations of a furniture company.*

In short, the first Leak tobacco factory was built in 1873 and is the one George P. Winfree refers to as being located on the back behind the old Leak home. Later, in 1884, Brown, Sapp & Co. built the large brick building on North Main Street that is now the oldest building of the Hooker complex. At some point, this structure was acquired by William H. Leak and operated as the W.H. Leak & Co. tobacco factory. About 1901, it was converted into a hosiery mill called Victor Knitting Mills, later called Victor Hosiery Mills.

William H. Leak and his younger brother James N. Leak were sons of Joseph H. Leak of Guilford County, North Carolina, and his wife, Mary A. Shaw, whom he married September 10, 1841. W.H. married Betty Pool and had several children, including Madye, who married John Marshall Pinnix

This page and next: Tags for plug tobacco produced by Leak Brothers & Hasten in Kernersville. Tobacco tags were used by manufacturers to identify their various brands. *Courtesy of Wayne Biby and Clarke Stephens.*

Sr. of Kernersville on September 22, 1904. This was the same year Pinnix obtained his North Carolina pharmacy license and opened his drugstore in Kernersville. Another daughter, Annie Leak, married Paul J. Nash Sr., and they were the parents of Pete Nash.

From various records, it appears the Victor Knitting Mill remained in business until about 1909. W.H. Leak died in Forsyth County December 4, 1915. Following its operation as a knitting mill, the old Leak tobacco factory was used to store furniture and was being used for that purpose in 1915. There were two furniture factories in operation in Kernersville at that time (Kernersville Furniture Manufacturing Co. and the Ring Furniture Company), so it is possible some of its inventory was stored in the old Leak factory building.

By 1923, the building was back in operation as a hosiery mill called Vance Knitting Co., and the original Leak tobacco factory building had been expanded by the addition of a large extension to the rear that included a dye room, boiler room and water closet. The building also had an open

The second building in the Hooker complex in a photo taken circa 1930 while it was still under construction. *Courtesy of Gloria Lowrey.*

elevator toward the front of the original part of the building. The Vance knitting mill was still in operation in 1933. Sometime between 1924 and 1934, a second brick building was added to the complex while it was still being operated by Vance. The second building was also two stories with a basement, as was the original.

After its operation as the Vance Knitting Co., Inc., the complex was acquired by Burlington Industries, at the time one of the world's leading producers of textiles and related items. It is believed Burlington moved into the building in April 1949 and remained there until January 1962.

In 1970, Hooker Furniture acquired the former Burlington Industries and Linwood Company plant in Kernersville. Not long after, this firm added the third brick building to the complex, just to the north of the original W.H. Leak building. After many years of operation, Hooker shut down its Kernersville furniture manufacturing operations in August 2003. Today, however, these buildings are once again being transformed, as the entire complex is being converted into commercial and residential space.

Kernersville Granite Works

Of the several types of minerals found in Forsyth County, granite is the most common in the eastern and southern sections, while the prevailing rocks throughout the western and northern sections are gneisses and schists. Granite occurs with some frequency in the area around Kernersville, and now-abandoned quarries can still be found there.

The *News & Farm* of July 23, 1885, had this to say:

> *Down near the depot there is quite a lively time just now, by a company of stone cutters from Winston, headed by Mr. C.A. McGalliard, preparing the rock steps for the new Methodist Church at Winston. It is said a company have leased Mr. J.W. Beard's Rock Quarry near town and are going to put up sheds and go into the business on a large scale. Today I was down there and one of the hands was missing and I asked what had become of him and some one said he was keeping "Blue Monday." I don't know what that means.*

In fact, historical records demonstrate that about 1885, Kernersville had its own granite yard located near the train depot, called McGalliard & Huske.

Robbins notes that granite, along with manufactured tobacco and dried fruits, constituted Kernersville's principal shipments in that day. He also records that J.W. Beard, one of the town's largest real estate and business

A party at the old rock quarry in Kernersville, circa 1900. Kernersville Bicentennial Book *photo, 1976.*

dealers and a partner in the firm of Beard & Roberts, "owns a quarry of superb granite, only a quarter of a mile from the depot, which he will sell or lease on easy terms to parties desiring to develop the same." His sketch continues: "The outcrop of granite in this vicinity is superb, and the sample monument, near our depot, with many tons that have been shipped, are the best of testimony as to its superior quality and capacity for splendid finish. Unlimited quarries are found here in close proximity to the depot, and present a fine field for development."

It seems likely the firm of McGalliard & Huske leased Beard's quarry for its enterprise. Its operation was described in glowing terms in an article entitled "Kernersville Granite Works," written in October 1887 by James Hubert Lindsay, editor of the *News & Farm*:

> *The granite monumental and building works situated at the depot has a very promising outlook. About two years ago the quarry was leased by Messrs. McGalliard & Huske, who determined to make a successful business out of it. They are well fixed with derrick, polishing engine and other modern appliances for hauling the heaviest material and doing the finest work. The granite is very fine indeed and is found in a ledge 12 feet thick. McGalliard & Huske are the only men in North Carolina, in the*

A picnic at the old rock quarry in Kernersville in July 1905. Kernersville Bicentennial Book *photo, 1971.*

business, who make a specialty of fine work, and Mr. C.A. McGalliard was the first man in the State to polish granite. There [sic] *orders in the last two years have come from all over the state. Among the orders filled have been the following:—granite for the new Methodist Church at Winston; for the Jewish Synagogue at Goldsboro; a fine monument to R.J. Reynolds in Winston, N.C.; granite for Y.H. Pegram's residence at Winston; granite for J.A. Gray's fine residence, Winston; monument to W.D. Stockton, Kernersville; polished cornerstone for Greensboro's Graded School building; monument to Thomas Crumpler, and O.G. Parsley, of Wilmington; a monument for the grave of W.P. Mast, Suffner, Fla.; and an order for a memorial tablet for the mother of Thomas Crews. The most recent is an order for a monument to be erected to the memory of Matthew Stack, a Moravian minister and the first missionary to Greenland. It will be put up in the Moravian cemetery at Bethabara, in this county.*

They always guarantee good work at fair prices as they can save buyers 25 per cent on freights and 25 on dealer's profits, when bought at the North. The granite is unexcelled anywhere. It submits to the very finest polish, which is an item of valuable consideration. Messrs. McGalliard & Huske deserve patronage. They are developing the resources of the State and transferring the rough, unpolished stone into a "thing of beauty." Such an enterprise is valuable to a State and should be encouraged by its citizens. As fast as it becomes necessary the force will be increased and all orders will receive prompt attention.

This notice is not paid for, as some might think. We have said what we have in the interest of an enterprise that is developing the State's resources and converting the raw, worthless material into that which is valuable. We trust you will place your orders for building or monumental work with McGalliard & Huske, of this place.

The same month Lindsay also wrote: "We are glad to learn that the work of putting up a monument to Missionary Stack has been awarded to Messrs.

Monument honoring Colonel Arthur Forbis, who died in the Battle of Guilford Courthouse in 1781. The inscription reads, "Presented by/ McGalliard & Huske/ July 4, 1887." *Photo by authors.*

McGalliard & Huske, of this place. No one is more deserving, nor would appreciate it more."

In January 1888, the *News & Farm* reported: "The granite quarried near the town is capable of the highest finish, and is not excelled by that quarried in any State. Orders are received for the granite from many sections of North Carolina and the surrounding States. Its reputation is growing and its superiority acknowledged." One such order was for a monument placed on the battlefield where the Battle of Guilford Courthouse was fought in March 1781 during the Revolution. It honors Colonel Arthur Forbes of Guilford County, who died from wounds received in the battle.

It appears the firm was still in full swing in April 1888, when a further snippet in the *News & Farm* added: "McGalliard & Huske are running a good force of hands at the Granite Works and are finishing up a beautiful work. The urn chiseled on the top of a monument that goes to Wilmington is very pretty in design and execution."

Despite these glowing acclamations, the company surprisingly shut down only a few months later. Why this enterprising business ceased operations is a mystery, although there is a possibility it was encountering financial difficulties. This clue comes from a final notice in the *News & Farm* printed June 22, 1888: "Mr. C.A. McGalliard, one of the proprietors of the Granite Works here, has moved with his family to Wilmington. Several creditors are left behind."

James M. Guyer House

A story in the Sunday, November 28, 1943 edition of the *Winston-Salem Journal and Sentinel* with the title "Arsenal, Hotel, Home of Mayor" describes the early history of a house that once sat on the west side of North Main Street, adjacent north to the Roberts-Justice house. It was widely known as the James M. Guyer house and, later, as Miss Mamie Guyer's boardinghouse.

According to Harvey Dinkins, the story's author, the Guyer house was used during the Civil War, when it "housed the gun works of S.H. Beard." The man dubbed "S.H. Beard" by Dinkins was probably Augustus H.S. Beard, who lived immediately south of the Roberts-Justice house. Again, quoting Dinkins: "When guns were no longer in such great demand as they were between 1861 and 1865, Dr. B.J. Sapp bought the rambling 10-room residence and operated it as a hotel."

While the house's early history has not been confirmed, it is known that it was eventually acquired by James Madison Guyer, a well-known Kernersville businessman and civic leader. As told by Dinkins:

> *J.M. Guyer purchased the property and remained its owner until his death in 1930. It was during the ownership of Mr. and Mrs. Guyer that the residence was best known, since Mr. Guyer was mayor of the town for many years, was cashier of Forsyth Bank and Trust Company in Kernersville at length, was a justice of the peace for years and was widely known as an insurance man for some time.*

It was in his capacity as justice of the peace that he was often called "Judge" Guyer.

James M. Guyer was born July 30, 1844, in Guilford County, North Carolina. He was the son of Jacob and Rebecca (Charles) Guyer; grandson of Nathan Guyer, who was born November 8, 1772, in Perquimans County, North Carolina; and great-grandson of Joseph Guyer, who married Miriam Bogue in Perquimans on April 5, 1769. It appears the Guyer family had Quaker connections in eastern North Carolina at this early date.

Exactly when Guyer arrived in Kernersville is unknown, but Forsyth's land records show that Haley and Sallie D. Davis conveyed a tract of land in Kernersville to Guyer in 1874. He must have done well because in 1877–78, he was mayor of the town. He was also a member of the firm of Beard & Guyer that was operating a general store there.

The 1880 census shows him living in Kernersville with his wife, Mary, and a stepdaughter named Sarah Poe. Mary had been previously married in Guilford County to James S. Poe, and Sarah was their daughter. Mary's maiden name was Bull, and she was born in Person County, North Carolina, the daughter of Jesse K. Bull and his wife, Dolly M. Long. While no record of the marriage of James M. Guyer to Mary (Bull) Poe has been found, it seems they were married sometime in the 1870s. The Forsyth County death records show that Mary Guyer died August 16, 1924, and was interred at Mount Gur Cemetery in Kernersville. Her tombstone gives her date of birth as July 24, 1840.

The 1900 census for Kernersville shows James M. Guyer living with his wife, Mary, and also a Mary C. Bull, age twenty, who is listed as his niece. There is no mention of the stepdaughter Sarah. This niece was actually Mary Cornelia Bull, the daughter of Jesse M. Bull and his wife, Mary Isabel McCuiston. She was born July 28, 1878. In later census records, Mary is referred to as "Mamie," and Dinkins says she was "best known as Miss Mamie Guyer, since she was the adopted daughter of Mr. and Mrs. Guyer." However, the fact that Mamie continued to be referred to as Mamie C. Bull in official records indicates that the adoption, if any, was not legally formalized.

"Judge" Guyer resided with Mamie until his death on October 14, 1930. In his will, he directed that his entire estate be sold and the proceeds divided as follows: half to Mamie C. Bull and the other half to Mrs. Sadie P. Leak, Mrs. Mabel Sterne, C. Elmer Leak and Herbert Leak, "share and share

The James M. Guyer house on North Main Street in Kernersville. *Photo by Sam F. Vance Jr., courtesy of his children.*

alike." However, during the administration of the estate, Mamie purchased the Guyer residence outright from the other heirs, and a deed was made by the executors conveying the property to her on November 22, 1937.

While she resided in the Guyer house, Mamie operated a boardinghouse there. The house itself was of two-story, four-bay, frame construction, with a long, covered front porch fronting on North Main Street. There was an exterior brick chimney at the south end and another, interior, brick chimney toward the north end, indicating the house was constructed in phases, as were many old houses. Dinkins had this to say about the dwelling: "The fact that it was constructed throughout of hand-dressed lumber, with framing put together with wooden pegs and with walls of inordinate thickness establishes the date at close to 100 years ago and possibly even further back than that."

The front porch of the house looked out over a yard filled with very large English boxwoods. Because of their size, they must have been quite old. Interestingly, when the executors conveyed the house to Mamie in 1937, the deed contained this clause: "There is expressly reserved from this conveyance all of the English boxwoods planted and growing upon said property, and the grantors specifically reserve the right, and such right and privilege is hereby granted by the grantee hereof, for the said executors to remove the same from the premises within two years from this date." So it would appear that there were others who had considerable interest in these stately plants.

When "Judge" Guyer died in 1930, a probate inventory of the contents of the house showed that it was sparsely furnished: "1 Bedroom Suit and 6 Chairs; 1 Chest of Drawers; 1 Bed and Bedding; 1 Small Linoleum Rug; 1 Organ; 2 Couches; 1 Sideboard; 1 Corner Cupboard; 2 Tables; 6 Chairs; 1 Refrigerator; 1 Kitchen Safe, Cook Table & Cooking Utensils; and 3 Porch Chairs." It is possible that two items of furniture pictured in the article by Dinkins—a walnut drop-leaf table and a walnut chest of drawers—were among the items enumerated in the Guyer estate.

During her tenure, residents of Mamie's boardinghouse could often be seen sitting in the rocking chairs that populated the long front porch. The house had another distinction, according to one of Kernersville's older residents: in one corner of the front yard stood one of the first public phones in town, where calls could be made for a nickel.

Mary Cornelia Bull died intestate on September 24, 1946, and was taken to Greensboro, in Guilford County, where she was buried in Green Hill Cemetery. She lies there today along with several of her relations.

The house remained in the possession of Mamie's heirs and their spouses for another twenty-two years, until it was finally sold on February 9, 1968, to Thomas E. Cooke and his wife, Frances S. Cooke. Not long afterward, the house was torn down and replaced by commercial property.

Davis Hotel

In earlier days, Kernersville had several small hotels and boardinghouses. They accommodated transient visitors, students who came to study there and those who came looking for work in the mills that sprang up during the late 1800s and early 1900s. As previously noted, Israel Kerner operated a hotel at the "Y" on South Main Street, while Dr. Benjamin J. Sapp operated Sapp's Hotel on the northeast corner of Main and Mountain Streets—it was renamed the Kernersville Auto Inn in the early 1900s. Even J.M. Pinnix is mentioned in some records as keeping boarders.

The Davis Hotel was another local hostelry that accommodated both short- and long-term residents. It stood on the west side of North Main, north of the James M. Guyer house. The hotel was a large, two-story frame structure with wraparound porches across the front on both floors. It was in operation by 1902 and was still standing in 1915. However, the building burned to the ground in 1918.

The owner of the hotel was Eurelius Grant Davis, son of Levi Franklin Davis and his wife, Louisa Phipps. Davis lived in the hotel with his family. Following the hotel's destruction, the Davis family constructed another two-story frame house across the street from the old one, where the northernmost building of the Hooker Furniture complex now stands.

E. Grant Davis was born in the Sandy Ridge section of Guilford County, North Carolina, on January 9, 1865. He attended Guilford County public schools and then Guilford College. He later transferred to the Oak Ridge

The ivy-covered building is the original Leak tobacco factory. The frame house to its left is the second E.G. Davis home. *Photo by Sam F. Vance Jr., courtesy of his children.*

Academy and graduated from that institution in 1882 after studying bookkeeping.

Following the completion of his schooling, E.G. moved to Kernersville, where his father, already a well-known businessman and leading citizen of the town, had served for nineteen years as mayor. There, in 1885, E.G. went into the dry goods, groceries and general merchandise business with his father, with the firm operating under the name L.F. Davis & Son. Their brick store was located on the north side of North Main Street just south and adjacent to the parking lot of the Musten and Crutchfield store. In 1919, fire gutted the store, but it was rebuilt within the same walls and still stands today. L.F. Davis also engaged in the real estate business and owned considerable property around the depot and along what is now Bodenhamer Street that he had surveyed into building lots.

On September 28, 1887, E.G. married Sallie Crews, daughter of a business partner, M.C. Crews, with whom he operated one of Kernersville's first hosiery mills—the Davis-Crews Knitting Mill. According to a notice in *Fibre and Fabric* magazine, it was organized sometime before November 18, 1899, and began business in a frame building on the corner of Bodenhamer and Burke Streets. It remained in operation until 1918, when Davis sold it to the owners of the Kernersville Knitting Mill, which became part of Adams-Millis Corporation in 1928.

Davis remained involved in various community and business enterprises until old age forced him to relinquish active business affairs. He died on May 1, 1941. According to a memorial of his life:

> *He retained his interest in the community in which he had spent the greater portion of his mature years. His health was considered good, particularly for one of his time of life. On Thursday of this week, feeling quite able to undertake such a trip, he went to Winston-Salem on business. While there he was stricken suddenly, and departed this life at the age of 76 years, 3 months and 22 days. He is survived by his devoted wife, Mrs. Sallie Davis, three daughters, Mrs. Carrie Whitaker of Charlotte, Mrs. Nellie King of Kernersville, and Mrs. Sadie Justice, also of Kernersville; by seven grandchildren, three great-grandchildren; and by two nieces, Mrs. Charlie Wrightson of Washington, D.C. and Mrs. Celetia Landers of Richmond, Va.*

The daughter Nell King lived in a large frame house directly across North Main Street from the Dr. James T. Justice house. This attractive house was later demolished to make room for an expansion of Main Street Baptist Church facilities. The daughter called Sadie Justice in the memorial was the second wife of Dr. James T. Justice, whom he married in 1932 following the death of his first wife, Minnie E. (Gold) Justice. Three other daughters were born to E.G. Davis and his wife; all predeceased their father.

A History of Kernersville Newspapers

In Robbins's 1888 sketch, we learn that the first newspaper published in Kernersville was the *News*. It was started by T.A. Lyon and H.C. Edwards, and the first issue appeared April 1, 1881, as a five-column folio. It was afterward enlarged to a six-column folio and finally to seven columns. It was printed on a small hand press.

The man called T.A. Lyon was Thomas A. Lyon Sr. He was born February 19, 1854, the son of John F. and Attelia Holden Lyon. His wife was Mildred Paschal. Sometime after Lyon sold his interest in the newspaper, he moved to Greensboro, North Carolina, where he died in 1941. He and his wife are both buried there in Green Hill Cemetery.

The other man mentioned by Robbins was Henry Clay Edwards. Born in 1832, he was the son of James Alpheus Edwards and his wife, Jane Meredith. H.C. Edwards married Nancy Josephine Boren, whose family later became prominent in the brick-making business in Greensboro. In addition to his interest in the *News*, Edwards was involved in several other commercial ventures in Kernersville in the 1880s. They included a sawmill and a general store called Edwards & Deen, both located near the depot. He was also proprietor of the first tobacco warehouse in Kernersville. It was called Farmers Warehouse and was originally located on Bodenhamer Street across from the old depot. It was later moved to a site closer to King Street, where it now stands. By 1896, Edwards was also a partner in Edwards & Stone, a canning business. His large, two-story brick home, completed about

The 1881 H.C. Edwards home in a photo taken circa 1895. Edwards is the bearded gentleman shown with a hat in his hand. *Courtesy of Richard B. Edwards Sr.*

1881, stands today on the north side of Route 150, across from the entrance to Smith-Edwards Road. Henry Clay died in 1915 and was buried in Mount Gur Cemetery. His son, Felix Marvin Edwards, was a prominent farmer who ran Elmwood Farm Dairy, delivering milk to customers throughout Kernersville and the surrounding area for many years.

Shortly after setting up their printing press, the two novice newspapermen found themselves in legal hot water. The difficulty stemmed from a story they published that led to a prosecution against them both for libel. The news piece that led to the difficulty stated in part:

> *A white man by the name of Alex Dean attempted rape upon a little girl of Mr. David Stocks, near Colfax, some time last week. A warrant was issued for Dean, and he was carried before J.A. Davis, Esq., justice of the peace. Squire Davis, after his style of dispensing justice, converts the case into an assault and battery, and discharges the offender of all decency and law upon payment of costs, which was $30. We presume that Mr. Davis had*

> *an eye to the fact that if this grave offender was bound over, or committed to jail, he would lose a handsome fee, and accordingly rendered his decision to suit his own convenience.*

Both criminal and civil proceedings were instituted by Davis against Lyon and Edwards, editor and publisher, respectively, of the *News*, on account of the publication. Both cases ultimately reached the North Carolina Supreme Court, where one was decided in favor of the defendants and the other against them. The legal aspects of the case were so interesting that it was included in a book, *Newspaper Libel: A Handbook for the Press*, published in Boston in 1888.

Perhaps the dust-up with Squire Davis convinced both Lyon and Edwards that the newspaper business involved more risk than reward, because both sold their interests in the paper to James H. Lindsay. An article written by Kernersville Moravian minister Reverend C.L. Rights in the July 24, 1883 edition of the *People's Press* had this comment:

> *The senior editor of the* News *has sold out to his partner and retired from the paper. Mr. Lyon deserves credit for inaugurating this enterprise in our midst, and the issuing of the first number of his paper should be*

Another view of the H.C. Edwards home from circa 1915, after the advent of electricity. *Courtesy of Richard B. Edwards Sr.*

> *commemorated as a "Red Letter Day" in the history of Kernersville, and only those having some knowledge of the difficulties of journalism, especially in the beginning, can fully enter into the merits of the question, especially when we remember that there were already four ably conducted papers in the county, before he started the* News, *and if, as it is asserted, newspapers are educators of the people, then we see we have made considerable progress since the day when Mr. John C. Blum made a similar venture in issuing the first number of his* Weekly Gleaner, *and its successors, for many years the only publication in the State west of Greensboro and Salisbury. In selling to Mr. Lindsay, we think Mr. Lyon has committed his "pet" into safe hands, as he seems to be in all respects a worthy young man.*

Robbins adds further details about the changes made by Lindsay after purchasing the *News*:

> *All the old type has been replaced by new—also new cases, stands and jobbing outfit added. A year ago by the aid of citizens, he secured a Campbell Power Press, to prevent his accepting a position elsewhere. There are printed at this office besides the* News, *the* Thomasville Gazette *and the* Summerfield Gleaner. *The job patronage has largely increased and it has become one of the best paying country papers in North Carolina. J.H. Lindsay has been unanimously re-elected Sec'y and Treas. of the N.C. Press Association three times in succession. He has been untiring in his zeal for the up-building of this place, but having been offered a lucrative position at Staunton, Va., will go there in a few days and leaves the field open here, for a good newspaper man.*

James Hubert Lindsay was a well-educated and highly regarded man. In his *Men of Mark of Virginia*, Lyon G. Tyler states that Lindsay was born at Casanova, Fauquier County, Virginia, December 29, 1862, the son of Silas Condit Lindsay, or Lindsley and Lindsly, as the name often appears in earlier generations. He was educated by his father and began teaching when he was only fifteen years old. He taught at the Staunton, Virginia Graded School and in Culpeper County, Virginia, read law and medicine privately and was a correspondent for several papers before moving to Kernersville. According to Tyler, Lindsay "purchased the *News*, a paper then losing money for its proprietors; greatly improved it, and made it a paying institution."

While in Kernersville, Lindsay also held the offices of town treasurer and postmaster, and a sketch written in 1886 adds that he was also a "dealer in cigars and confectioneries." On December 24, 1884, Lindsay married Annie R. Sieg. The same year, he was elected secretary and treasurer of the North Carolina Press Association, holding office in that organization until he left Kernersville to take a position in the School for the Deaf and Blind in Staunton, Virginia. Afterward, he moved to Charlottesville, in Albemarle County, Virginia, where, in 1890, he founded the *Daily Progress*, a newspaper still in circulation in that city. In 1900, he was selected to serve in the Virginia constitutional convention held in 1901–2. Lindsay and his wife, Annie, were still living in Albemarle in 1930, according to census records.

Silas Condit Lindsay was also a prominent individual. A native of New Jersey, he attended Princeton University, where he graduated with a BA in 1828. He also attended the Princeton Seminary, graduating with an MA in 1829. Upon graduation, he moved to North Carolina to take charge of the Oxford Academy in the town of that name. Three years later, he moved to Greensboro, where he became a professor of Latin at the famed Caldwell Institute, a Presbyterian school. S.C. Lindsay himself was a Presbyterian minister. Silas C. Lindsay married Amelia G. Spottswood. In the 1880s, he followed his son to Kernersville, where he served for a while as principal of the Kernersville Academy. During this time, Mrs. R.F. Lindsay was assistant principal and Mrs. J.H. Lindsay served as a teacher of music and art at the school.

The *News* was mentioned again in an item in the *People's Press* of February 19, 1885, written by Reverend C.L. Rights:

> *The* Kernersville News *is going to have a new home some of these days. The editor has purchased a building from Mr. Haley Davis, and uncle George Stewart has the contract for moving it across the street to the lot bought for it. At present, however, the concern is stuck, not in the mud, but in the snow, and Mr. Lindsay must possess himself in patience till better weather, which is not so hard as he has a young wife to sympathize with him and sing, When all our trouble will be over for him,—but when he gets fixed he will have a nice office.*

According to the 1886 edition of Branson's *North Carolina Business Directory*, the paper was a "Dem. Weekly," meaning it supported the Democrat political position.

Sometime before October 7, 1887, Lindsay renamed his paper, calling it the *News & Farm*. The earliest known issue still existing was published on October 7, 1887, and the last appeared on July 6, 1888. At about this same time, Lindsay also began publishing a monthly literary magazine at Kernersville called the *Southern Home* that described itself as "devoted to pure literature and general home reading." It cost two dollars per year. Only one issue is known to exist—July 1, 1887.

In 1888, the *News & Farm* ceased publication, and the name was changed again to the *News*. The earliest and last known issue of this version of the paper appeared on November 2, 1888. It named J.H. Lindsay as editor and stated that it was "devoted to literature, news, politics, agriculture, education and southern progress."

Lindsay must have departed for Virginia soon after this name change, because the 1890 *North Carolina Business Directory* lists the paper but credits W.C. Stafford and H.L. Coble as the editors and proprietors.

The old Kernersville High School (later called Kernersville Academy) was built by a stock company, opening in 1858. However, in the late 1870s, it was operated by the Methodist Episcopal Church, South as a "conference" school. Professor H.L. Coble came to Kernersville from Randolph County to take charge of the conference school in 1888, according to an item in the April 27, 1888 edition of the *News & Farm*: "Dr. W. Coble, father of Prof. H.L. Coble, who will take charge of the High School next session, was in town for a few days, this week. While here he rented a portion of Mr. E.J. Stafford's residence, opposite the Academy, to be occupied by his son about the first of July."

According to Robbins, Coble "comes highly recommended, and will endeavor to put the school on an elevated plane, so that Kernersville will offer not only one of the sightliest [*sic*], healthiest and most pleasant locations in the State, but high educational, moral and social advantages," as well. So, it seems Coble also dabbled in the newspaper business as well as serving as principal of the Kernersville Academy. William Cornelious Stafford, born in 1858, was the son of Francis Marion Stafford and his wife, Sarah Elizabeth Teague. W.C., who married Florence E. Rights in 1879, was a well-known businessman and civic leader around Kernersville and, for many years, operated the W.C. Stafford store on North Main Street.

Stafford and Coble must have found the newspaper business unprofitable, because they sold out sometime before 1891 to Thomas Joseph Robertson.

According to a biography in a *History of North Carolina*, he was born at Bachelor's Hall in Pittsylvania County, Virginia, the son of John M. Robertson. About 1876, John M. moved to North Carolina, locating near Kernersville. He was a farmer for many years but later moved into the town of Kernersville and went on the road as a salesman. According to the biography:

> *Thomas J. Robertson attended rural schools while his father lived on a farm, and was also educated partly in the Kernersville Academy. He has had experience in practically no other trade or profession than printing or newspaper work. At the age of seventeen he began an apprenticeship in the Kernersville Printing Office. In 1888 he became foreman of the* Burlington News *office, remaining there for three years, after which he returned to Kernersville and bought the* News. *After publishing that for a year he leased the* North Wilkesboro News *for three years, and in 1896 established the* Hustler, *which live and popular journal he published ten years.*

Robertson did not operate the paper for long before selling it to James Arthur Holloman. Evidence for this appears in the October 7, 1892 edition of the *Daily Herald* of Brownsville, Texas. The article "How a Brave Young Lady Eloped with a Newspaper Man" is amusing reading:

> *Raleigh, N.C., Oct. 7—James A. Holloman, news editor of the* Raleigh State Chronicle *and editor of the* Kernersville News *was at 3:20 o'clock yesterday morning married at the Yarboro hotel here to Minnie Kerner, a pretty girl of Kernersville and a member of a prominent family.*
>
> *Thus ended an elopement which was planned by the lady herself. For months they have been engaged but Miss Kerner's parents set their faces sternly against a marriage and Holloman could no longer visit his fiancé. Two months ago they planned an elopement. A mutual friend procured a marriage license in Forsyth county one night and Holloman went there from here but in some mysterious way the brothers of Miss Kerner ascertained the fact that a license was issued and that night took her to Virginia, going from resort to resort in that State. Holloman did not know for a considerable time what state she was in.*
>
> *A few days ago she returned home. Day before yesterday Holloman went to Kernersville to make a democratic speech. He did not see Miss Kerner and had no means of arranging for an elopement. As his train, bound*

> *for Raleigh, left Kernersville last night Miss Kerner was standing on the platform of the station between her mother and father. She was dressed in a tennis costume.*
>
> *As the last car was passing her, moving quite rapidly, she made a spring at the platform and in an instant was gone before her parents could raise a hand.*
>
> *The trip to Raleigh was uneventful. On their arrival here at 2 o'clock this morning the registar* [sic] *of deeds was roused from the bed and hurried to his office, where a license was issued. A preacher was also secured in the same speedy way and in the hotel parlor in the presence of a party of newspaper, telegraph and hotel people, the groom and her* [sic] *plucky bride were united, the latter wearing her picturesque tennis costume.*

The young lady was Minnie Gertrude Kerner. Born in Kernersville in 1870, she was the daughter of Richard P. Kerner and his wife, Auleno Flynt. Her husband, James A. Hollomon, went on to an illustrious career in journalism. According to the January 7, 1918 edition of the *Constitution*, a well-known Atlanta, Georgia newspaper, "James A. Hollomon, one of the south's best known newspapermen, will, beginning today, be in charge of *The Constitution*'s news bureau in Washington." Hollomon later became an associate editor of the *Constitution*, a position he held until January 1929, when he died from injuries sustained in a fall down a stairway at the Henry Grady Hotel in Atlanta. Following a very large funeral there, Hollomon's body was returned to Kernersville for burial in the Main Street Methodist Cemetery.

The next owner of the *News* was Virgil Guyer, according to the December 15, 1892 issue of the *Landmark* of Statesville, North Carolina: "J.A. Hollomon has sold the Kernersville *News* to Virgil Guyer, a young man of High Point, who will assume editorial management at once." No further information on Guyer has been found other than the fact that he must have sold his interest in the *News* sometime before April 21, 1895, according to an amusing snippet that made its way into the *Washington Times* on that date: "Last fall a newspaper man named George F. Shafer, from New York state, came to Kernersville and purchased the *News*, a weekly paper, which he has since been publishing. Thursday night he moved his property to an unoccupied house on the outskirts of town. Since that time he has been missing. His whereabouts is unknown." The *Landmark* added that Shafer skipped town, "leaving several creditors to mourn him." How a New Yorker came to buy the paper is anyone's guess.

The 1895 edition of the *Ninth Annual Report of the Bureau of Labor Statistics* for North Carolina lists only one Kernersville newspaper: the *Silver Advocate*. The editors were Anderson and Anderson. It was a weekly, published on Friday, with one dollar being the cost of an annual subscription. This paper is also listed in *North Carolina and its Resources*, published in Raleigh, North Carolina, in 1896. Branson's business directory for 1896 also cites Anderson and Anderson as editors of the *Silver Advocate*. The paper was still in business in 1897 according to the *Eleventh Annual Report of the Bureau of Labor Statistics*, which calls it a Democrat weekly with W.E. Anderson as editor. William E. Anderson is listed in the 1900 Kernersville census as "Book Agent," but no further information on him has been found. Research indicates there were other newspapers in the United States in 1896 called the *Silver Advocate*, and it seems they supported William Jennings Bryan in the U.S. presidential race of 1896. In that race, Republican William McKinley, representing the gold side, defeated Bryan, who was a silver advocate, and this is likely the origin of the name of the papers of that name. No issues of Kernersville's *Silver Advocate* remain, but there is an item from the paper that was reprinted in a Winston-Salem paper. It was a "card" inserted in the paper by Mrs. Robert Jordan of Kernersville bemoaning the death of her husband and son in a shootout with revenue agents in their home in Kernersville in March 1896.

While it seems the *Kernersville News* was not published in 1895, it resumed publication in 1896 according to Branson's, which lists the editors and proprietors as W.C. Stafford and H.L. Coble, again calling it a Democratic weekly paper. Why these two gentlemen repurchased the paper is a mystery.

This second venture by Stafford and Coble did not last long either, because the *Twelfth Annual Report of the Bureau of Labor Statistics* for 1898 lists only one newspaper in Kernersville, the *Messenger*. Its editor was H.E. Shore, and the owner was listed as J.F. Kerner. The latter was James Frederick Kerner, who was born in 1871. His wife was Eva Maud Sapp, daughter of Newell Wesley and sister to Zora Bessie Sapp, who married Kernersville physician Dr. J.R. Paddison Jr. The paper was printed weekly, on Thursday, at an annual subscription cost of one dollar. No copies of the paper are known to exist. H.E. Shore was Henry E. Shore, who was born in 1855 and died in November 1919. He was the son of Wiley F. and Sarah L. (Williams) Shore. Henry married Nancy Ella Kerner, daughter of Dr. Elias Kerner and his wife, Parthia Gazelle Dicks. He became postmaster for Kernersville on June 12, 1897, a position he held until June 5, 1901, when he turned that duty over to Branson R. Beeson. According to the 1900 census, James F. Kerner was listed as a merchant and Shore as postmaster, so it's possible the paper was out of print by that date.

While it is not clear how long the *Messenger* lasted, it was certainly out of print by 1901, since it was not listed in the *North Carolina Year Book* of that date. In fact, according to its data, Kernersville had no newspaper until 1908, when it is credited with one called the *Forsyth News*, whose editor was T.J. Lowry. Lowry also published the *Surry Visitor* of Mount Airy in the 1870s and 1880s and the *Yadkin Valley News* of the same city in the late 1800s.

Lowry did not remain in Kernersville; the editor of the *Forsyth News* for the years 1909 through 1914 was a man named F.A. Slate. This was Frances Augustin Slate, who was born September 25, 1866, and died November 10, 1954. In 1900, Slate was living in Meadows Township, Stokes County, North Carolina, where he was operating a lumber mill. However, the 1910 census shows Slate and his family living in Kernersville and his occupation as newspaper publisher.

Slate sold his interest in the paper sometime before November 1915 to William Porter, who became its editor. His name also appears in the 1916 *North Carolina Yearbook* in the same capacity. One of the authors owns a copy of part of a page from the *News* printed in November 1915 that has this short item: "Ninety-eight years ago last Thursday, Nov. 18 Mr. Joseph Kerner moved from Friedland to Kernersville and located where the Auto Inn now stands. The weather was cold and drizzly just as it was on the ninety eighth anniversary."

William Porter was a Methodist minister who was born April 11, 1873, and died December 26, 1944. His first wife was Letitia Cockerham, whom he married in 1895. They had three children: Thurman Allen Porter (born November 16, 1895), Garland Burns Porter (born June 3, 1897) and Willie Letitia Porter (born November 10, 1901). Letitia died a few days after the birth of their daughter.

According to a private communication from Mrs. Lee Porter, wife of Garland Burns Porter Jr., when William Porter first moved to Kernersville as minister of the Methodist Protestant Church, he lived in the home of W.S. Linville of Kernersville. On August 8, 1906, Porter remarried, this time to Annie Auleno Kerner. She was a sister to Minnie Kerner, who married James A. Hollomon. At some point, Reverend Porter decided to change careers, and after studying law, he became an attorney in Kernersville. According to

Mrs. Lee Porter, after their marriage, William and his wife, Annie, lived in the old Richard P. Kerner home on South Main Street in Kernersville that was recently demolished.

William's son, Garland Burns Porter Sr., attended the University of North Carolina at Chapel Hill, where he became a close friend of the famous North Carolina novelist Thomas Wolfe. In a private communication with one of the authors, Garland Burns Porter Jr. noted, "My father and Thomas Wolfe became friends while they were students at UNC and kept in touch with one another thereafter. I remember Thomas Wolfe visiting our home in Atlanta around 1935 because my father told me Mr. Wolfe was not walking on stilts, but actually was that tall." This visit is recounted in the book *Thomas Wolfe Interviewed 1929–1938*, by Aldo P. Magi and Richard Walser:

> *In Atlanta on his way to New Orleans, he* [Wolfe] *stopped just long enough to get in touch with two college friends from Chapel Hill days, Ernest Henry Abernethy and Garland B. Porter, and to promise them a visit on his return. After Biloxi, Wolfe headed northeast to keep his promise… At Garland B. Porter's home, Dinner the first evening was typical North Carolina fare: fried chicken, snap beans cooked with a slab of streak-of-fat-streak-of-lean, candied yams, fruit salad, and plenty of biscuits and gravy. Wolfe consumed several bountiful servings. He told Porter and his family, "You've got to excuse me, but this is the first real meal I've had in years—this is the kind of food I was raised on."*

Garland B. Porter Sr. was very successful at Chapel Hill, where he graduated with a BA in 1923 and an MA in 1924. While a student there, he served as the first president of the student body, according to the May 23, 1921 issue of the *Landmark* headlined "Garland B. Porter Made President of the Student Body." He went on to a successful career in journalism as a reporter for the *Winston-Salem Journal*, southern advertising manager for Hearst and, at one time, that company's director of its North Carolina news bureau. Later, he became general manager of *Southern Advertising and Publishing* in Atlanta.

The *North Carolina Yearbook* lists William Porter as editor of the *Forsyth News* for 1916, but when it ceased publication is not known, as no issues of the *Yearbook* were published for the years 1917 to 1921. The 1922 and 1923 issues of the *Yearbook* show papers published in Winston-Salem but none in Kernersville.

Given the lack of further information on newspapers in Kernersville during the 1920s and early 1930s, it seems likely that the town was without one until 1935, when a paper called the *Forsyth Liberal* appeared. It was a weekly paper whose editor was Paul Swanson. According to the Library of Congress's Chronicling America project, the earliest known issue is dated August 4, 1939, and the last known issue is dated January 5, 1940. A curious note about Swanson appeared in the Miami, Florida *News* on January 6, 1936, under the headline "Editor in Carolina Faces Arson Count." The story, datelined Winston-Salem, reads as follows: "Paul Swanson, 31, local attorney, editor and owner of the *Kernersville Keeler*, weekly paper, was in jail at High Point awaiting trial on a charge of arson. Swanson was arrested here yesterday and was taken to High Point, where a warrant had been issued at the instigation of Monroe Tate, tenant in a house owned by Swanson. Tate charged Swanson set fire to the dwelling Saturday night while it was occupied." Nothing further of either Swanson or the paper referred to as the *Keeler* is known.

Sometime in 1938, an enterprising young man named Frederick Preston Carter came to Kernersville and began publishing the paper that is still known today as the *Kernersville News*. He was the son of Frank M. Carter and his wife, Jennie Smith.

According to an obituary from the *Kernersville News* published January 16, 1975, and copied below, Carter "came to Kernersville in March 1938 to take over the job as managing editor of the *News* which had been established by A.C. Huneycutt of Mocksville," in Davie County. So, the paper was already in existence when Carter arrived. However, a year later, he became its owner and editor.

Fred Carter died January 10, 1975. Sometime later, John F. Owensby, who had married Carter's daughter Connie on June 10, 1970, took over publication of the *News*, and he remains its owner and editor today. Carter's obituary reads as follows:

> *Fred Preston Carter, 61, editor and publisher of the* Kernersville News *and president of Carter Publishing Co. Inc., died about 5 p.m. Friday at Central Carolina Grocers Inc. after suffering a massive heart attack.*
>
> *Mr. Carter and his son-in-law, John Owensby, were in process of delivering a piece of furniture to the grocery firm when he was stricken. Members of Beeson Crossroads Rescue Squad and Dr. Richard H.*

Whitaker were on the scene within a few minutes but all their efforts failed to elicit any response from the victim.

Mr. Carter was a native of Davie County. He came to Kernersville in March 1938 to take over the job as managing editor of the Kernersville News *which had been established by A.C. Huneycutt of Mocksville.*

Fourteen months later, on April 13, 1939, Mr. Carter's name appeared in the masthead as "Editor and Owner." He continued to have the paper printed in the Mocksville plant until the July 4, 1940 issue which was the first to be produced in his own shop. Those early years were a constant struggle with Mr. Carter almost a one-man newspaper, with Mrs. Ruth Carter, his wife, his assistant.

As the community grew, the newspaper prospered and in 1963, he moved into the present building at 300 E. Mountain St. At the same time, a newer press, capable of producing, cutting and folding an eight-page section, was installed.

This served the newspaper's needs until May 20, 1971 when the paper switched to offset reproduction and the printing was "farmed out" to the Eden News *where it is now being printed.*

Last December, the Board of Directors voted to purchase a four-unit 16-page offset press which is now in process of being installed. It was his dream to have his own modern plant in order to provide the best paper possible for the community.

He was a member of First Baptist Church where he taught the Men's Bible class 15 years and served as an usher. He was also a member of the Board of Directors of the July 4th Celebration and one of its strongest supporters. He was a member of the Lions Club, the Chamber of Commerce and the Winston-Salem Moose Lodge. He was an organizer and charter member of the Kernersville Exchange Club and served as a state director.

Funeral was held at 3 p.m. Sunday at First Baptist Church with his pastor, the Rev. Amis Daniel and the Rev. Homer Good officiating, and burial was in Oaklawn Memorial Gardens in Winston-Salem.

Survivors include the widow, Mrs. Ruth Smith Carter; one daughter, Mrs. John (Connie) Owensby of Kernersville; one son, Frederick P. Carter of Kernersville; and two brothers, Hix Carter of Winston-Salem and Hubert Carter of Mocksville, and two grandchildren and one step-granddaughter.

There were two other papers published in Kernersville. One was called the *Leader*, but there are no known issues still existing and nothing is known about it other than that it was probably published before the modern *Kernersville News* went into operation in the late 1930s.

The second was a small paper called the *People's News*, published in the 1950s by Pete Nash, who ran a printing shop in Kernersville. A weekly paper, it was given away free. As noted earlier, Nash lived in the old Leak house, now demolished, and his printing shop was located in one end of the house. Nash's paper contained many interesting stories about Kernersville history gleaned from natives of the town who had firsthand experience with the incidents they recounted. Nash died November 3, 1974, and is buried at Main Street United Methodist Church.

The Early Banks of Kernersville

The Bank of Kernersville, the town's first bank, was chartered by the North Carolina General Assembly during its 1893 session. It was authorized to issue capital stock in an amount not to exceed

> *one hundred thousand dollars, divided into shares of twenty-five dollars each, and that for the purpose of receiving subscription for said stock, books shall be opened at any time after the ratification of this act and remain open for the space of sixty days at Kernersville, under the superintendence of the following persons or a majority of them, to-wit: Tyre Glenn, J.C. Roberts, J.M. Greenfield, L.F. Davis, W.H. Leak, W.A. Lowry, B.A. Brown, J.N. Leak and J.M. Guyer, and such other places under the superintendence of such other persons as said commissions may direct.*

Although the act was ratified on March 6, 1893, it seems that insufficient shares were subscribed to actually bring the bank into operation, and it was not until January 1, 1903, that it opened for business. It was established by Walter Hill Mendenhall and W.S. Linville. Mendenhall was born May 20, 1877, six miles north of High Point, North Carolina, in the Deep River area. George V. Fulp, the cashier, was the son of William Walker and Laura Ann (Vance) Fulp. He was born July 22, 1874.

In its first year, the bank had capital stock valued at $15,000 and was housed in a two-story brick building—still standing—that occupied the southwest corner of Main and Mountain Streets in town.

An early photo of the Bank of Kernersville building. *Photo by Sam F. Vance Jr., courtesy of his children.*

W. H. Mendenhall, President. Geo. V. Fulp, Cashier

The Bank of Kernersville

JUN 24 1903

Kernersville, N. C., 190

Mr Lee Roy Rumley.

Bank of Kernersville letterhead from 1903 showing W.H. Mendenhall, president, and George V. Fulp, cashier. *Courtesy of Wayne Biby.*

According to the October 1904 edition of *Telephone Magazine*, Kernersville's first telephone company operated on the bank's second floor. Its original incorporators were W.C. Linville, George V. Fulp, M.V. Fulp, F.W. Lubert and A.N. Linville.

In 1903, the bank's assets totaled $23,042, a figure that grew to $77,473 in 1907, $92,194 in 1912 and $125,541 in 1914.

George V. Fulp Sr. and his sons Willard, George and Paul played an important role in the development of the bank into a sound financial institution. According to published accounts, in 1933, when other banks were locking their doors during the deepening Depression that gripped the country, the bank kept its doors open and continued to do business until the federal government ordered all banks closed on March 6. However, it reopened soon after, on April 7, 1933, and remained in business thereafter until 1965, when it merged with Wachovia Bank.

Encouraged by the success enjoyed by the town's first bank, a second financial institution—Forsyth Bank and Trust Company—opened in 1906.

George V. Fulp, the Bank of Kernersville's first cashier, later became president, a position he held for many years. Kernersville Bicentennial Book *photo, 1971.*

According to the *Greensboro Record*, J. Van Lindley of Pomona, a community near Greensboro, was elected its president and James M. Guyer cashier. It was located on North Main Street, not far from where the old Auto Inn (originally Dobson's Tavern) stood.

Lindley, the driving force in setting up the bank, was born November 5, 1838. He was the son of Joshua Lindley, who was a fruit grower and nurseryman in Guilford County, a line of work his son followed with great success. In 1866, following the end of the Civil War, J. Van or "John," as he was known to his family, established the New Garden Nursery, also known as Joshua Lindley & Son. Business prospered, and in 1877, John began business as sole proprietor of the Pomona Nursery. It eventually expanded into North Carolina's leading nursery and cut flower business. Lindley was also a civic leader of Guilford County and a businessman with many varied interests. He became president of the Underwriters' Fire Insurance Company of Greensboro and of the Security Life and Annuity Company, also of that city. He was also a director of many businesses in Guilford County and elsewhere in North Carolina.

Forsyth Bank and Trust was considerably smaller than the Bank of Kernersville. In 1906, its assets totaled $13,844, far short of the $76,768 sported by the latter institution. By 1907, its assets had grown to $21,909. However, its fortunes seem to have declined because by 1912, its total assets had dwindled to $11,318, a figure that declined further to $8,923 in 1914. It is believed that the bank closed its doors soon after.

It is possible that the bank's dwindling fortune was due to the fact that it was robbed in February 1909 by one of Kernersville's own citizens, a quiet, solitary young fellow named Gaither Bodenhamer. It seems that Guyer went to lunch and left the vault open, which appears to have been his usual practice and was not considered especially odd, since the bank was located on the town's busiest street. Bodenhamer was watching this transpire and, as soon as Guyer was out of the way, forced the front door open, took the cash from the vault and strolled quietly out of the bank. He was soon apprehended, and the stolen money was returned to the bank, but it is likely many citizens in the town decided it was safer to put their hard-earned money into another bank.

It seems Lindley left the bank sometime before 1912, because in that year, D.W. Harmon is listed as president. In 1914, the last year for which records of the bank can be found, James M. Guyer is listed as president and R.S. Nelson was cashier.

The Great Storm of 1893

On August 15, 1893, a tropical storm formed in the Atlantic Ocean to the east of the Cape Verde Islands. According to modern analyses of records made at the time, it passed through the islands on August 16. While crossing the Atlantic headed toward the Lesser Antilles, the storm grew into a major hurricane on August 18. It continued to strengthen as it crossed open water, reaching Category 3 status on August 22. Three days later, on the evening of Friday, August 25, the storm's track began to deviate from its westerly course and arched west-northwest.

As it approached the Florida coast, its effects began to be felt in the Sea Islands—the chain of tidal and barrier islands that lie along the coasts of Florida, Georgia and South Carolina—with the winds increasing steadily during the night of August 25.

Eventually, the storm turned northward, moving roughly parallel to the coast for about one hundred miles and then making landfall near Savannah, Georgia, on August 27. According to contemporary reports, wind speed during landfall was about 120 miles per hour. Barometric pressure in Savannah was measured at 960 millibars; modern estimates put the pressure around 954 millibars at landfall and possibly as low as 931 millibars out at sea, which would have made it a Category 3 hurricane at impact. After making landfall, its center passed between Augusta, Georgia, and Columbia, South Carolina, as it curved up the eastern seaboard.

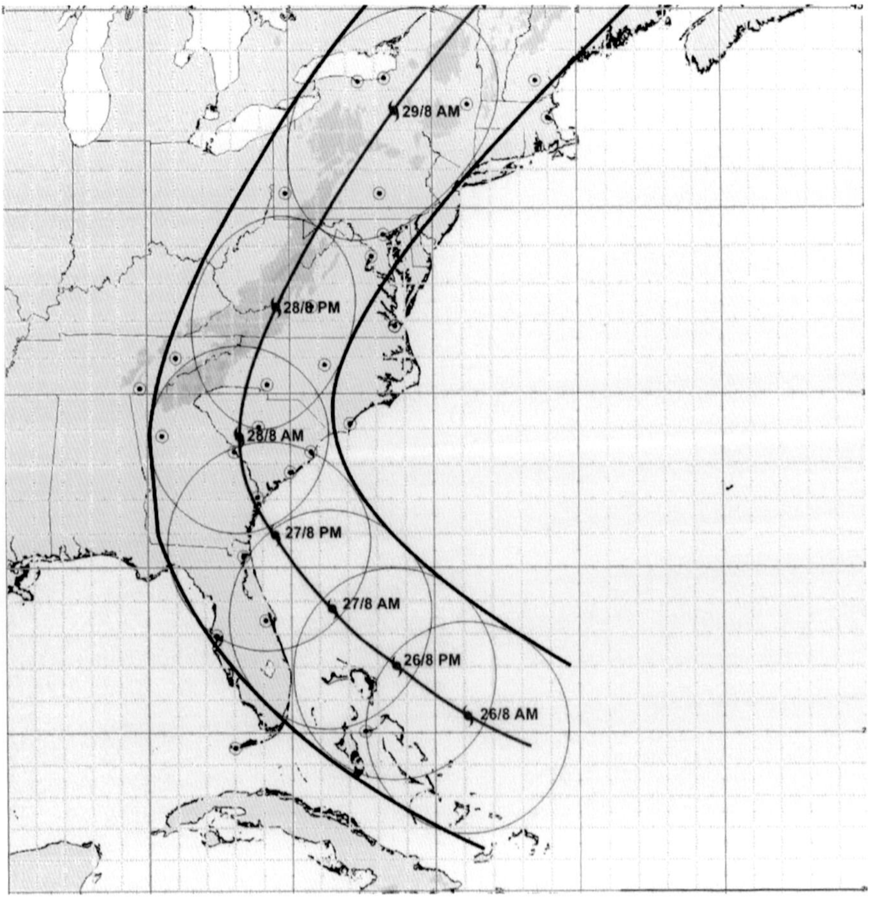

Track of the 1893 Great Sea Island Hurricane showing the swath of the one-thousand-millibar contour. *Courtesy of National Oceanic and Atmospheric Administration.*

According to *Storm Tides in Twelve Tropical Cyclones (Including Four Intense New England Hurricanes)* by Brian Jarvinen, a former researcher at the National Hurricane Center, the storm was one of the largest to strike the Atlantic Coast when measured by the radius of its one-thousand-millibar contour—it was much larger than Hurricane Hugo, which devastated Charleston in 1989, although not as intense at landfall.

With wind gusts as high as 120 miles per hour and a storm surge of between twelve and sixteen feet, the worst effects of the hurricane struck the Sea Islands near Beaufort, South Carolina. At the time, these islands were almost entirely populated by former slaves of the Gullah language and culture. With no advance warning of the impending disaster and no means of evacuation, some two thousand people died in the storm, and more than seventy thousand were left totally destitute in coastal South Carolina and Georgia.

This storm—known today at the "Great Sea Island Hurricane"—caused extensive wind damage to most counties in South Carolina and in many parts of eastern Georgia before moving on to North Carolina and other states in the mid-Atlantic.

In the southern part of North Carolina, wind from the storm created wide-ranging structural and crop damage, but havoc was not confined to that region, as other towns and counties in the state were also hard hit. One of these was Kernersville. Hurricanes are accompanied by weather conditions that produce tornadoes (or cyclones, as they were called in earlier times). From the evidence, it seems probable that much of the damage sustained by Kernersville was the result of such a cyclone.

One of the first newspapers to report on the hurricane damage was the August 30, 1893 *Greensboro Patriot*, which carried a story under the banner "A Fearful Storm: Houses Unroofed and Considerable Damage Done." According to the paper, "The oldest citizens in Guilford County cannot remember a storm equal to the one which struck this section on Monday and lasted all day. Strange to say, however, little damage to property was done to Greensboro although fences were thrown down and limbs of trees literally cover the ground." The story continued: "At Kernersville, a barn was blown down and a horse pinioned underneath the timbers but the horse was taken out without much injury. A barn belonging to Mr. Wesley Sapp was also unroofed, and a negro house in the suburbs was blown down and a child was killed and its parents were injured. The Baptist Church, a brick structure was also torn down by the wind."

Reports mentioned in the same story from elsewhere in Guilford County painted a grim picture of what the paper called "fearful destruction to tobacco and corn." The *New York Times* of August 30, 1893, also carried numerous accounts of storm damage along the entire eastern seaboard of the United States, including a brief mention of the damage at Kernersville:

> *A terrific cyclone struck here at 5 o'clock this morning. Nearly 100 houses were wrecked and a woman was killed. Many were injured.*
>
> *The Baptist, brick church was razed to the ground. Factories, stores, and residences were unroofed and some were blown entirely away. High winds and heavy rain are still raging.*

The *Times* then proceeded to catalogue a number of other reports it had received, which collectively demonstrated the extensive damage wrought by the storm as it spiraled up the Atlantic coast. The paper included the following notices on damage in North Carolina, among many others:

> *Wilmington, N.C., Aug. 29.—The Norwegian bark* Bonita *was blown ashore in the gale which prevailed here yesterday and today.*
>
> *The schooner* B.I. Hazard, *Capt. Rafford, Georgetown, for Elizabethport, N.J. with a cargo of railroad ties, put in at Southport this morning, in distress, leaking, and with spanker and mainsail lost.*
>
> *The brigantine* Wastrow *(German) Liverpool for this port, with a cargo of salt, went to pieces on Caswell Beach. The crew saved themselves by swimming ashore. They are now at the Caswell life-saving station.*
>
> *An unknown three-masted schooner is also reported ashore, leaking and showing signals of distress, on the same beach, two miles southwest of Southport. The life-saving crew has gone to her assistance.*
>
> *The three-masted schooner* Three Sisters, *with a cargo of lumber from Savannah for Philadelphia, was wrecked and abandoned on Cape Fear on the night of Aug. 28. Her commander, Capt. Isaac Simpson of Market Hook, Penn., and Mate Johnson Heede of Park Avenue, Baltimore, were washed overboard and drowned. The survivors are: William Simpson, steward, brother of the Captain; John Washington, John Scott, and another man, name not known. The vessel was left anchored in a leaking condition.*
>
> *Beaufort, N.C., Aug. 29.—The schooner* Amelia P. Schmid *is under Cape Lookout for harbor. A three-masted schooner, unknown, with lost sails, is flying flags for immediate assistance off the bar; also an unknown large vessel, mast gone, supposed to be square rigged, is flying colors of distress. The bar is impassable and for some time assistance cannot be rendered. Merritt's wrecking organization has been notified that large quantities of lumber, two water casks, and spars from a square-rigger have washed ashore.*
>
> *Raleigh, N.C., Aug. 29.—A terrific Storm of wind and rain raged yesterday from the seaboard to the mountains. It began Sunday and came from the north-east. There was but little rain during Sunday night, but the wind blew a gale.*
>
> *Throughout the cotton belt the wind and rain have done great damage. The plants have been blown down and the bolls have been beaten off. It is impossible now to estimate the loss, but it must be one-fourth the crop.*

> *The track of the storm, both wind and rain, appears to have struck along the northeast portion of the State and reached the Raleigh and Gaston Railroad just north of Henderson.*
>
> *The damage to all crops along this route is very severe. At Oxford the wind was strong enough to blow down a brick tobacco warehouse.*
>
> *From Oxford the storm swept on through Granville County, Rockingham County, and into Forsythe* [sic] *County, gathering in velocity until it became a veritable cyclone when it reached the town of Kernersville, which was wrecked.*

On August 31, the *Statesville Landmark* weighed in on the storm with numerous accounts of damage, one mentioning Kernersville. According to the paper, "The storm of last Sunday evening and Monday extended all along the Atlantic coast. It had its origin in the West Indies and moved slowly northward, leaving death and destruction in its path. The damage to life and property can hardly be estimated." An example included in the piece was a warehouse at Oxford blown down. The *Landmark* detailed damage to Kernersville in a separate story called "The Cyclone at Kernersville," which was a firsthand account based on information from Dr. Carey Sapp, a Statesville dentist and former Kernersville native:

> *Dr. C.C. Sapp, of Statesville was at Kernersville during the cyclone Monday, and left soon after it was over. He says the barn of his father, Dr. B.J. Sapp, was blown down but none of his stock was injured. One horse was caught between the rafters when the roof fell and held fast. It was necessary to cut the timber away in order to get him out, but the animal was unhurt. In addition to the damage reported by our Kernersville correspondent, the mill of Dr. E. Kerner, west of town, one of the largest in that section of the country, was completely wrecked, together with several outbuildings. Lowery, whose tobacco factory was unroofed, is the father-in-law of Mr. E.J. Stafford, of Statesville, and he writes Mr. Stafford that several hundred boxes of his tobacco were damaged. Will Phillips, colored, who works for Mr. Stafford, is a son of Monroe Phillips, whose house was demolished, his wife injured and his foster-daughter killed. Will received a telegram Monday informing him of the occurrence. Dr. Sapp wired* The Landmark *Monday afternoon that 40 or 50 houses were seriously damaged and that the total loss is estimated at $25,000.*

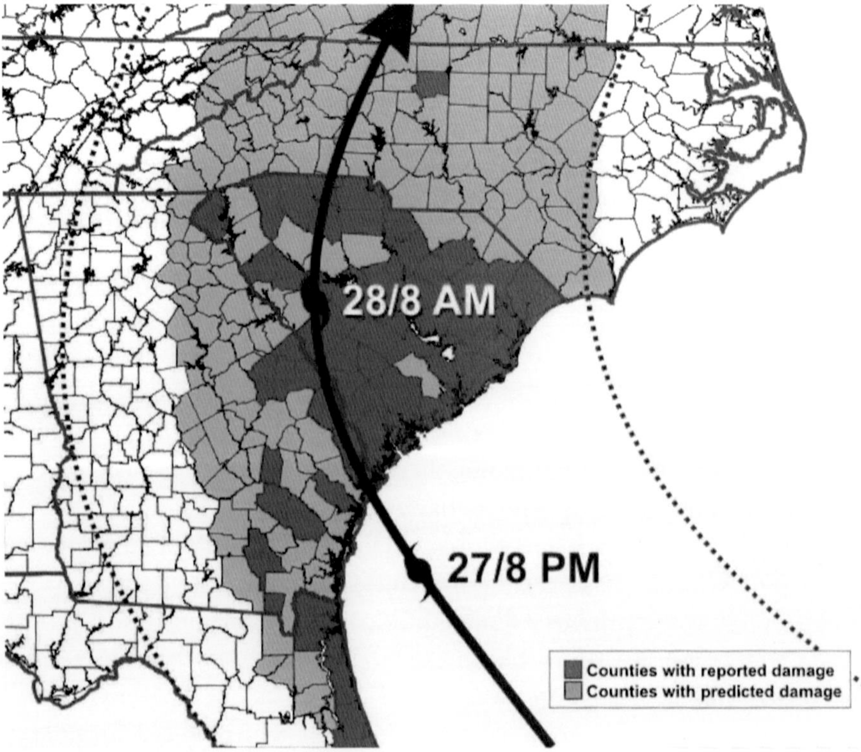

Reported and predicted (by National Hurricane Center models) damage from the 1893 storm. Dotted lines indicate bounds of one-thousand-millibar contour. *Courtesy of National Oceanic and Atmospheric Administration.*

The Dr. Kerner mentioned in the *Landmark* story was Dr. Elias Kerner. In 1876, he and his father, John Frederick, erected a saw- and gristmill about a mile west of the town, probably the one wrecked by the cyclone.

The August 31, 1893 *Landmark* also carried a report of the storm by a gentleman named J. Henry Tharpe, who was working in Kernersville as a principal at the Free School there when the storm struck. His account, datelined Kernersville, August 28, 1893, appeared under the following headline:

> *STORM SWEPT KERNERSVILLE*
> *A Storm Passes Over the Town and Demolishes in its Path*
> *One Person Killed and Others Injured*
> *An Iredell Man Who was There Tells about It*

Last Thursday morning bright and early, I took the train for this place to begin my school again, but owing to the scarcity of money met with little success. I believe I would have succeeded notwithstanding the hard times, which are keenly felt here, had it not been for the calamity which befell the town this morning in the form of a cyclone. Such a scene has never been witnessed in this country.

At about 4:30 am, while most of the town was taking its morning nap, a terrible wind and rain storm struck the town right in the centre destroying almost everything in its path. The track of the cyclone is about 400 yards wide, coming almost directly from the east. It first struck C.T. Snider's house and that of Monroe Phillips colored, a half mile east of town. Snider's house is a large brick dwelling. The end struck by the storm was blown in catching his daughter and holding her in bed until the rubbish could be removed. Phillips house was a good frame building but was literally demolished. A child he had taken to raise was killed and his wife was at point of death from fright and wounds received by falling timbers. Phillips is a darkey, but is a good citizen and thrifty. The storm came on into town, blowing down trees, barns and everything in its path. Messrs Fulp & Linville the largest merchants here suffered a heavy loss. The roof of their building was entirely blown away and their goods are lying in the rain except what have been moved out. Hands have been working faithfully all day to save them but no estimate can be made of the damage.

Mrs. Sallie Davis' house a good frame building was unroofed and the main part of the upper story torn away. A large frame building occupied by Mr. Caraway and his mother in law Mrs. Leak was almost ruined. The end occupied by Mr. Caraway was torn away nearly to the ground, while the other end was not damaged. J. W. Leak's residence was damaged greatly by the chimney toppling upon the roof and crushing it in. His large grain barn was completely demolished, but his horses five in all, were unhurt. The Baptist church, which has been completed but a short time and the largest church in the place, is a complete wreck. It was a brick structure and is demolished down to the foundation. A total loss of over $2000. A number of barns were blown down with out houses and shops of every kind. Mr. Gid Kerner's house is a total wreck.

Strange to say amid all the destruction none were seriously hurt except those already named. It was fortunate that the storm came in the night, for had it been in day time people would have rushed into the streets and been killed by the flying timbers. Those who were in it say it lasted about two minutes.

George Ray suffers a large loss. His barn was new he having lost his old one last spring by fire and it is down to the very bottom rock. In it he had hay and forage enough to winter his three mules and cattle, two wagons, two buggies, mowers, wheat drill, corn planter and other things all of which are a complete loss. His mules escaped but one is badly hurt. It swept over his tobacco and did not leave a whole leaf in the field. The barns of Dr. Sapp, N.W. Sapp, J.W. Leak, L.W. Fulton and J.W. Beard beside those already named are complete wrecks. The academy is damaged so that no school can be taught until a considerable amount of work is done on it the roof being broken through. The old public school house was swept in splinters from the face of the earth but the new one just in the edge of the storm was not damaged.

Beard & Roberts store was partly unroofed and also Lowry & Son's tobacco factory. But one chimney was left standing above the house tops in the path of the cyclone. No estimate can be made of the damage. Not a fence or out house, tree, stalk of corn, plant of tobacco, or any thing is left where the storm swept. The writer has never witnessed such before and hopes he may never again for so terrible was it that the half can never be told. It is now 2:30 pm and the wind has not ceased to blow nor the rain to fall in torrents for a minute today. The streets are flooded but the people work manfully to save the property exposed.

According to 1900 census records, William Caraway, his wife, Nannie, and her mother, Mary Leak, were residing in Kernersville at the old W.H. Leak home where Pete Nash later lived.

The Baptist church struck by the cyclone stood at the corner of West Mountain and South Cherry Street. According to church records, it was chartered on August 30, 1884, by a group of seven women and three men who met that day: John Hepler and wife, H.P. Moore and wife, Charles Lipscomb, Mrs. Rebecca Carter, Mrs. B.A. Brown, Mrs. Virginia Stockton, Mrs. Lucy Kirk and Mrs. Lacy Ann Lemar. In 1885, $674.02 was set aside for building, and an additional $803.53 was added in 1886, the year the one-story brick church destroyed by the storm was erected.

From various studies of the Great Sea Island Hurricane of 1893, it seems the eye of the storm passed well to the west of Forsyth County sometime on the morning of August 28. This put Kernersville in the damaging northeast quadrant,

A 1922 photo of Huff's Garage (originally the W.A. Lowery & Son tobacco factory), one of many buildings unroofed by the 1893 storm. Kernersville Bicentennial Book *photo, 1971.*

an area notorious for spawning tornadoes. All indications are that a damaging tornado did occur early on that Monday and approached the town from the east, heading in a southwesterly direction. Many of the structures mentioned in the various press accounts were scattered along both sides of South Main Street in the town but mainly south of its intersection with Mountain Street.

While the Great Storm of 1893 had a major impact on Kernersville, efforts were quickly commenced to repair the structural damage created. Mr. Tharpe, the *Landmark* correspondent who had written earlier about the damage, penned another of his "Notes from Kernersville" in the October 19, 1893 edition of that paper that showed that recovery efforts were well underway and life was once again settling back into its normal pace. His letter, dated October 16, seems a fitting conclusion to the story of the storm:

> *Our town has about recovered from the effects of the cyclone of August 28. All the unroofed houses have been re-roofed and all the chimneys rebuilt, but the signs of the storm are visible yet.*
>
> *The Baptists have their new church up ready for the roof and the work goes rapidly on. This is a gratification to all, for the loss of their church was a sad loss to them.*

The Blue Ridge Conference of the M.P. Church met last Thursday with Mt. Pleasant church, four miles from Winston, on the Norfolk & Western Railroad, Bishop Jno. F. Hurst, of Washington, presiding. Rev. C.W. Smith, of Harmony, Iredell county, is returned as presiding elder of the Statesville district, and on Harmony circuit Rev. A.J. Johnson succeeds Rev. J.H. Patterson, who goes to the sea coast. On Yadkinville circuit Rev. D.S. George is returned.

The fever in our town has about subsided.

Plenty of frost this morning. Respectfully, J. Henry Tharpe. Kernersville, N.C., Oct. 16, 1893.

Two Conflagrations at Kernersville Graded School

According to the *Kernersville Bicentennial Book*, a public or free school was opened in Kernersville in October 1892 and stood next to property that is today occupied by the Pierce-Jefferson Funeral Home on the corner of Cherry and West Mountain Streets. The school's first principal was J. Henry Tharpe of Statesville, mentioned in the previous story. The following description of the school was provided by a former student, Mrs. W.G. (Carrie Winfree) Cooke, wife of former Kernersville magistrate and mayor Will Cooke:

> *It had the Big Room and the Little Room. Prof. Henry Tharpe was principal and Miss Nan Bodenhamer was teacher for the lower classes (1, 2, 3, and 4. No grades. They "progressed" by books). They started with the Primer. The others were in the first, second, third and fourth readers. They attended six months—from October until March. Their lessons were recited on the recitation bench in front of the class facing the principal or teacher, whose desk was on a platform (approximately 6 by 10) across the front of the room. The children sat in double desks and their recitation bench was about the length of the platform. Mr. Tharpe taught algebra, history, geography, Latin and French. Four other teachers were: Add N. Linville, George Fulp, Sr., Miss Sue Galloway, and Gid Hastings. Mr. Tharpe taught summer school and it was called a "Subscription School." There was a charge of approximately $3 per month. Miss Alie Fulton taught in the summer of 1894 and Miss Bodenhamer taught in the summer of 1895.*

Others who taught at this school included Reverend J.W. Pinnix, who later served as principal, Miss Mary McKaughan, Miss Lucy Perry and a Mr. Chitwood.

In 1905, the general assembly of North Carolina passed a law entitled "An Act to Establish a Graded School in the Town of Kernersville, Forsyth County, North Carolina." It created a public school district called the Kernersville School District. It also provided for a Board of Graded School Trustees, with five members to be elected at the first regular municipal election of the town of Kernersville following ratification of the law, which was on the first Monday in May 1905. The first trustees of the graded school were W.S. Linville, J.M. Greenfield, L.F. Davis, Dr. W.C. Ashworth and D.W. Harmon. The act also authorized the Board of Commissioners of the town to levy an annual tax "of not more than fifty cents on the one hundred dollar evaluation of property in said school district and not more than one dollar and fifty cents on the poll in said school district for the support and maintenance of the graded school in said district." In addition, the law vested all existing public school property in the new graded school, including that belonging to the public or free school mentioned above.

In March 1905, the Kernersville Public School held its final closing exercises, an event described by C.T. Snider in the *Western Sentinel* of March 30, 1905:

> *KERNERSVILLE, March 27—One of the most successful, pleasant and delightful commencements that has ever been given in Kernersville took place on Friday, March 24. It was the closing exercises of said school taught by Rev. J.W. Pinnix, principal, who is one of the most progressive teachers in the State, assisted by Mrs. W.M. Hepler and Miss Annie Lowery.*
>
> *The address of welcome by Clay Ring was well delivered and brought forth cheers from the large audience present.*
>
> *The declamations and dialogues were of a high order from the beginning to the close. Mrs. Hepler presented three nice prizes to three of her pupils, and the gifts were highly appreciated.*
>
> *Miss Annie Lowery also presented three handsome prizes to three of her pupils. Then came four large and beautiful prizes from the principal. The first was presented by Rev. Mr. Porter to Miss Mattie Bodenhamer, for the greatest progress in Arithmetic. Two prizes were given to Miss Myrtle Thornlow for the largest number of head-marks. The last prizes were*

presented by Prof. Ingraham to Miss Annie Snider for the greatest progress in English grammar, and Miss Mary Trent for the greatest general progress.

The principal then made a brief but appropriate address on the school and the work accomplished during the past session.

This was followed by the valedictory by Charlie Albert, who charmed and captivated the entire audience.

Then closed perhaps the most successful session of Kernersville public schools ever taught in this town.

The sermon at night in the Methodist church by Rev. Mr. Porter was one of the best and most appropriate ever heard here.

As required by the legislation creating the new Kernersville graded school, the free school was taken over in the fall of 1905, and the graded school commenced operation despite a legal controversy over several provisions of the law creating it. The case—*Lowery et al. v. Board of Graded School Trustees in Town of Kernersville*—ultimately made its way to the North Carolina Supreme Court but did not prevent the school opening as planned in the fall of 1905.

Unfortunately, the new public school did not last very long. According to the *Kernersville Bicentennial Book*, shortly before the end of the 1906 spring term, it burned to the ground. So when the fall term began, the school was relocated to the old Kernersville Academy building, which had been closed the previous year, and continued there through the spring of 1907 while a new facility was being constructed.

So it seems that the graded school initially opened in the old public or free school building and continued there until the fire, while plans were underway to build a new school. In fact, on March 8, 1906, the Kernersville graded school trustees purchased a one-acre lot in town for the new school building. It was purchased from Dr. Carey C. Sapp and M. Vance Fulp. The deed notes that the property was known as the J.S. Ray property and consisted of a one-acre lot that adjoined the Kernersville Academy, Main Street, Cherry Street and the John F. Kerner property. The academy (old Kernersville High School) stood in the geographic center of town, so the school lot was located nearby, which would place it close to where S&R Motor Company stands today—a marker there today marks the original town center. Interestingly, the graded school fire took place just a few days after the deed was drawn.

The conflagration is described in an article that appeared in the *Western Sentinel* on March 15, 1906:

FIRE IN KERNERSVILLE
Graded School is Destroyed by Flames Last Night—Other Notes.

KERNERSVILLE, March 7—Last night about 11:30 o'clock the public school building here, in which is being conducted the graded school, was burned to the ground.

It was discovered to be on fire by some young men going in the direction of Oak Ridge. They returned to town and gave the alarm. It being a frame building the flames spread very rapidly and the entire structure was completely destroyed in 30 or 40 minutes after being discovered.

Only a small number of the citizens knew anything of the fire until this morning. Heroic efforts were successful in saving the frame barn of H.E. Shore, which stood in 50 feet of the school building. As quick as thought, Mr. Odell Beard was on the roof amid the shower of sparks and burning shingles, throwing water, and others in the barn sprinkling the dry fodder and catching the sparks as they would fall through the roof.

While the origin of the fire is not known it is thought to have caught from the stove in which fire was left when school closed in the evening.

The building cost about $1200 and was comparatively new, having been erected only a few years ago. The loss to the town is quite severe at this time when funds were needed to successfully operate the new graded school. This of course will necessitate the closing of the graded school as there is no other building suitable for the work in the town. At this writing the writer has no statement from the principal of the school or the trustees.

At the time of the fire, H.E. Shore owned the house that is now part of Pierce-Jefferson Funeral home, confirming the fact that the original graded school was located close by. Marvin Odell Beard, also mentioned in the story, lived nearby on Cherry Street.

Planning for the new school must have begun soon after the fire, as the school trustees quickly moved to acquire property for a new building. This time they purchased a two-acre tract of land. According to the deed made July 16, 1906, the grantors were children of Newell Wesley Sapp of Kernersville and their spouses.

From the land description provided in the deed, it appears that the property was located on the Greensboro Road (now East Mountain Street) close to where Kernersville Town Hall stands today. Why the trustees did

Photo of the second Kernersville Public School. Built in 1906, the school burned on the night of December 31, 1925. Kernersville Bicentennial Book *photo, 1971.*

not use the land they had purchased on South Main Street is unknown. Perhaps they decided to build a more substantial school and felt more land was needed. In any case, construction of the new school commenced soon after the land was acquired and was finished in time for the 1907 fall session.

The new structure was a handsome, two-story brick building with a cupola on top that housed the bell that had previously belonged to Kernersville Academy. It accommodated both graded and high school students. The first principal of the school was Reverend Henry Wenhold (1907–8), pastor of the Kernersville Moravian Church. Other principals who served at the school included Professor J.M. Weatherly (1908–9), Professor W. Speas (1909–10), Professor McKeown (1910–11), Professor Arnold Hall (1913–14), Professor Tillet Hendrix (1914–15), Professor Rowe (1917–18), Professor J.M. Weatherly (1919–21) and Professor R.A. Sullivan (1921–27).

In December 1925, the school recessed for the Christmas holiday, no doubt pleasing all the students in attendance. Then, while the school was shuttered, tragedy struck in the form of another fire. It began on the evening of December 31, New Year's Eve, and before it was extinguished, it had consumed most of the structure. The event is recalled in the *Kernersville Bicentennial Book*:

> *The most tragic event in the history of education in Kernersville was the fire that destroyed the Kernersville School on December 31, 1925. The fire was discovered about 8:30 p.m. when flames were seen coming from the*

Class photo taken circa 1919 of students on the steps of the second Kernersville public school building. *Courtesy of Nell Marshall.*

> *roof of the building. Such headway had been gained that the fire fighting apparatus of this city was unable to check the wild spread of the flames and fire fighters from Winston-Salem were asked to come over. Both fire departments brought the fire under control. According to the* Twin City Sentinel *of January 1, 1926, "Damage of more than $40,000 was done to the graded and high school building and equipment in this city last night when fire destroyed the entire front part of the building and part of the new addition, which was completed about three years ago." About $25,500 insurance was carried on the building and equipment.*

Another account of the conflagration appeared in the *Greensboro Daily News* on New Year's Day 1926 and provides additional details of what happened:

> *KERNERSVILLE SCHOOL BUILDING DESTROYED*
> *Fire sweeps Through Structure,*
> *Causing Loss of About $40,000*
> *Insurance of $25,000*
> *(Special to Daily News)*

Kernersville, Dec. 31.—Fire discovered about 8:15 o'clock tonight virtually destroyed the graded and high school buildings at this place. The blaze burned furiously for more than two hours, it being about 10:43 o'clock before it was gotten under control. Fire chief Nissen, of the Winston-Salem fire department, brought a truck and aided the local fire fighters in subduing the flames.

Although a small portion of the structure is still standing, the part that remains was considerably damaged and tonight it was not thought likely that the building could be repaired to the extent that any of it might be used again. The loss tonight was estimated at around $40,000, with $25,000 insurance.

Origin of the fire is somewhat of a mystery. It appeared, when first discovered, that the blaze started in or near the roof, although so far as is known no fire had been in the building since school closed for the holidays. The flames were bursting through the roof when discovered.

The building was of brick construction. Half of it was built about 20 years ago but improvements to the structure had made it a modern school building, accommodating 550 pupils and a teaching force of 19. The school met all the requirements for the standard "A" grade.

Tonight it was impossible to say what arrangements might be made for carrying on the work of the school. There are no buildings in the town which might be occupied temporarily. The school was to have re-opened Monday following the holiday recess.

The *Greensboro Patriot* of January 4, 1926, also covered the story. It also noted that the origin of the fire was a mystery, especially since it seemed to have started on the roof. An account in the *Kernersville News* of February 4, 1970, given to the paper by then Kernersville fire chief Ned Stuart, stated, "Although the fire almost completely gutted the inside of the building, the firemen did manage to save a twelve room structure a short distance away."

A few former students of the school still live in Kernersville today, and more than one of them believes the fire was a case of arson. Some believe they know who the culprits were. This is how the *Patriot* characterized the fire:

School Is Burned at Kernersville
Five Hundred Fifty Students and 19 Teachers Idle
Is Damage of More Than $40,000.

Ralph A. Sullivan, principal of the Kernersville Public School when it burned in 1925. Kernersville Bicentennial Book *photo, 1971.*

The largest fire in the history of Kernersville destroyed half the graded and high school building here on Thursday night, ending the study activities of 550 students and the employment of 19 teachers temporarily and doing damage in excess of $40,000.

Flames were noticed about the room at 8:15 o'clock, but had gained such headway that the local company could not cope with them, and the Winston-Salem fire department was called upon. It immediately dispatched a company which rendered valiant service in bringing the fire under control and preventing nearby residences from igniting. Until the Winston company arrived the local company fought well, and the new water system, which has just been installed, perhaps prevented the entire building from being reduced to ashes.

The building was valued at $75,000. It was insured for $25,000.

Four rooms of the building which were constructed as a part of a new fireproof addition to eight rooms built 20 years ago, were saved but damaged by fire and water. The beautiful auditorium was completely destroyed. It is believed that the four rooms saved can be put in usable condition, but authorities were unable to say what they would do with students and teachers now.

Forsyth county was to have taken over the school today, which taught as high as eleventh grade; but the public is in a quandary as to whether the town or county will act to solve the situation.

Origin of the fire is unknown. No fire had been in the furnace of the building since Sunday.

Under the guidance of Prof. R.A. Sullivan, superintendent, the school had become one of the most efficient in this section of the state, in the opinion of patrons of the school.

Because there was no single building in town that could be pressed into service as a temporary school, the students were fanned out to different places. According to the *Kernersville Bicentennial Book*, at a meeting of the Forsyth County Board of Education held on January 2, 1926, a plan was approved to "have their high school taken to Walkertown, two grades to Sedge Garden, and the remainder of the grades to be handled in their present temporary buildings, the Junior Order Hall and the Methodist

Photo of the LaFrance fire truck purchased by the town of Kernersville in 1923. *Courtesy of Gloria Lowrey.*

Episcopal Church South." At that time, plans had already been made for the county to take over the Kernersville grade and high school system. J.R. Blackwell Jr., a former teacher at the school, said that he taught in the shell of the old building after the fire. It was later renovated, and shacks were built as temporary school room accommodations.

The fire proved a major inconvenience to almost everyone in town: students, parents and teachers alike. Fortunately, the Forsyth County Board of Education acted quickly to build a new school, purchasing twenty-eight acres of land on West Mountain Street in March 1926. According to the book *Kernersville High School Remembered: 1927–1962*, the property was purchased from the Linville family at "$10 per foot front for the depth of 200 feet; $4,500 for a 100 foot frontage with a bungalow on it; and $370 per acre for the ground to the rear extending back to the Southern Railway right-of-way." Soon after the purchase, architectural drawings were completed and construction commenced. "By the spring of 1927, the auditorium at the new campus had been completed and the members of the class of 1927, who had completed their senior year at Walkertown held their graduation ceremony in the new auditorium." Construction proceeded apace, and the entire school was completed in time for students to go there for the fall session of 1927.

The new school served the town for decades, but like the others before, it too met its end. This time, however, it was the wrecker's ball that claimed it and not fire. A new school, Kernersville Elementary, stands on the site today.

The Burning of the American Hosiery Mill

Economic activity in Kernersville boomed following the arrival of the railroad in 1873, and tobacco was the economic staple. The mercantile trade also thrived, and businessmen like James William Beard and John Calvin Roberts made good money. Beard was the son of William Asbury Beard and his wife, Martha Henley, daughter of John Henley. He was born September 22, 1841, and died October 19, 1897. His wife was Susan Jane Phillips.

According to Robbins, Beard was a Davidson County native who came to Kernersville about 1866 and engaged in the real estate business. Over time, he acquired substantial landholdings in town and offered free lots to any who would erect substantial factories on them. About 1873, Beard built a two-story brick residence on the east side of South Main Street, but it was taken down in the 1950s when Dr. Richard Whitaker purchased the site for a medical office building.

John Calvin Roberts was born in February 1833 and died August 12, 1909. About 1874, he became a partner with Beard in the firm of Beard & Roberts, and in 1879, the two men erected a large, two-story, brick store in town. Robbins described it as a building 26 by 112 feet in dimension, "filled with a very complete assortment in all lines of general merchandise, comprising dry-goods, clothing, boots and shoes, hats, groceries and grocer's drugs, hardware, notions, house furnishing and everything properly coining under this general heading." Their trade was largely in "country produce, dried fruits and berries for shipment." An ad for the firm in the April 27,

Drawing by Leroy Wagner of the Beard & Roberts tobacco factory taken from an old photo made in 1909. *Courtesy of Leroy Wagner.*

1888 edition of the *News & Farm* recited that Beard & Roberts "Carry the Largest and most Attractive Stock of Goods in Town. Ready Made Clothing, Boots and Shoes, Groceries, Drugs [and] all are invited to call and examine our mammoth stock of new goods."

In 1874, Roberts built a large, two-story brick house on North Main Street that later belonged to Kernersville physician Dr. James T. Justice.

In 1880, Beard & Roberts expanded its business ventures to include the manufacture of plug and twist tobacco. The new business prospered, and in 1884, the partners decided to construct a new tobacco factory on the corner of Beard and East Railroad Streets in Kernersville. Of brick construction, the structure was 52 by 136 feet, with five floors, making it the largest factory in the town in those days. According to Robbins:

> *The annual output* [of the factory] *has been from 100,000 to 150,000* [pounds of tobacco], *requiring the services of 50 to 75 hands in its production. The trade as with other dealers is largely in the South and "Beard's Favorite" is widely known among dealers. "Sweet Relief," "Piedmont Beauty," "Old Gold," and several other popular brands are on their old list and with the present year they have started a new brand called "Red Devon," which is designed as a superior chew.*

This page: Tags for plug tobacco brands produced in Kernersville by Beard & Roberts and Lowery, Son & Company. *Courtesy of Clarke Stephens.*

The men continued in business together until Beard died on October 19, 1897. His will devised his interests in his merchandising and manufacturing partnership with Roberts to his children.

Beard's partner, John Calvin Roberts, died in Kernersville on August 12, 1909. His will left his half interest in the Beard & Roberts tobacco factory to his wife. Perhaps not as well known as Roberts's business activities was his extensive involvement in the affairs of the Methodist Church in North Carolina. This work earned him a place in Powell's *Dictionary of North Carolina Biography*. Importantly, his generosity was instrumental in bringing High Point College (now High Point University) into being, a point widely heralded in the media of the day, including mention in the August 20, 1909 edition of the *Washington Post* under the banner: "$10,000 For Church College." Roberts's biographical entry reads as follows:

> *(February 1833; 12 Aug. 1909), active Methodist Protestant layman and benefactor of Kernersville,* [Roberts] *was a member of the board of trustees of the Methodist Protestant Publishing House in Greensboro and was almost singularly responsible for the impetus given to the efforts of the Reverend J.F. McCulloch in the early twentieth century to establish a Methodist Protestant college in North Carolina. Roberts was a charter member of the Kernersville Methodist Protestant Church, organized in 1884, and took part in all its activities, serving for many years as Sunday school superintendent and class leader.*
>
> *At the meeting of the North Carolina Annual Conference of the Methodist Protestant church in 1901, Roberts offered $10,000 to be used for the establishment of a denominational college in the state and a special Ways and Means Committee of nine persons was appointed. Due to the economic conditions surrounding the panic of 1907, however, efforts to establish the school were postponed. When Roberts died two years later, he left the $10,000 bequest in his will; the bequest stipulated that the funds be used by the Conference Board of Education in the building for support of a college provided that it was opened by 1920. If not, the money was to be used as a trust fund and the income applied towards educating young men for the ministry.*

Following the deaths of both partners, their tobacco factory building was purchased by Orah W. and John G. Kerner, sons of Richard P. Kerner, operating as the American Hosiery Mills. The mill had operated from 1904 to 1910 under the name American Knitting Mills before becoming the American Hosiery Mills, perhaps about the time the Kerner brothers acquired the Beard & Roberts factory. While not proven, it seems likely the Kerners leased the factory building before purchasing it.

John G. and Orah Kerner with employees of their American Hosiery Mills company in a photo taken circa 1915. *Courtesy of Nettie Hester.*

Whatever the case, disaster struck the mill on the morning of April 15, 1912, when a fire broke out on the third floor and quickly spread, consuming most of the structure. A story of the conflagration appeared the following day in the *Greensboro Daily News* of April 16, 1912, under the headline "The Hosiery Mill at Kernersville Burned." The report carried this account:

> *Kernersville, April 15.—The American Hosiery mill owned by O.W. and J.G. Kerner was destroyed here today by fire. The fire originated on the third floor from some unknown cause. It was discovered about 11 o'clock and within ten minutes the entire floor was in a blaze. All of the employees some 60 in number escaped unhurt. Something like 12 or 15 knitting machines, worth possibly $250 each were removed from the building. A part of the wall on the east end of the factory fell,* [and] *while all the other walls are standing they are so swerved from the intense heat that they are expected to fall any moment.*
>
> *The loss will doubtless total $65,000 or $70,000 with very little insurance. Messrs Kerner Brothers have just recently purchased the building from the estates of J.C. Roberts and J.W. Beard.*
>
> *A row of six tenant houses situated near the factory, belonging to Dr. C.C. Sapp, were saved by the use of a Chemical engine the town purchased last fall.*
>
> *Information as to whether the mill would be rebuilt could not be gotten definitely.*
>
> *The Postal Telegraph office was situated in the factory building and managed by Mr. John G. Kerner.*

The *Washington Post* also carried a notice of the fire in its April 12, 1912 edition that simply noted, "The $100,000 hosiery plant and dry house of the American Hosiery Mills at Kernersville were burned at noon today."

Interestingly, the Kerner brothers tried to recoup their losses by blaming the fire on a passing locomotive engine belonging to the Southern Railway Company, claiming it threw a spark that ignited the fire. In an effort to back up their claim, they filed suit in Forsyth County Superior Court, but the court rejected the plaintiffs' claim in an opinion rendered during its May 1914 term. Unhappy with the result, the Kerners appealed to the North Carolina Supreme Court on November 17, 1915. In the case *O.W. Kerner v. Southern Railway Company*, Justice Brown summed up the basics of the appeal as follows:

> *The action is brought to recover damages for the destruction of the plaintiff's factory in the town of Kernersville 15 April, 1912.*
>
> *The plaintiff offered evidence tending to prove that a freight train of the defendant, with an engine in charge of John Snyder, was defective as to its spark arrester and was so unskillfully operated that it emitted large quantities of live sparks which set fire to inflammable material in the plaintiff's factory and destroyed it. The defendant introduced evidence to the contrary. The jury found the first issue in favor of the defendant.*

According to the court, at the trial plaintiffs offered to prove that "two weeks after the fire, after dark, one of the plaintiffs was at the ruins of the burned factory and that a train was coming from Greensboro, and that as the engine passed it threw live sparks from its smokestack which fell where the burned building formerly stood." However, the trial judge excluded this evidence as there was no other evidence offered to prove that it was the same engine operated by Snyder at the time the fire started. That engine, identified as No. 123, was attached to a freight train driven by Snyder. In rejecting the evidence, the court said, "To prove that the engine referred to, not 123, threw sparks two weeks afterwards on the site of the burned factory is no evidence that 123 threw sparks on the factory and set it afire on 15 April, 1912." In short, the court rejected all of the plaintiffs' assignments of error and affirmed the opinion of the lower court.

About 1912, the Kerner brothers erected a new brick building on the site where the former Beard & Roberts factory was located and were again doing business as American Hosiery Mills Company. The plant continued to operate until 1921, when it was idled. Sometime between that date and April 1924, the building was converted to a warehouse and utilized by Southern Railway to store freight. In later years, it was occupied by various manufacturing companies that reworked and expanded the building to meet their growing needs. They included Birdsboro Steel Corporation, which produced a product called Mirawal at the plant during the 1950s and 1960s. Mirawal was a porcelain-coated, painted steel that came in various colors. Later, the building was taken over by the industrial fabrics division of Burlington Industries, which operated there until 1988, when the company sold the division to Takata Corporation. Today, that company operates it as the Highland Industries finishing plant, specializing in industrial fabrics.

Orah W. Kerner died in Kernersville on November 6, 1923. His obituary appeared in the *Atlanta Constitution* the following day:

> *James A. Hollomon Tuesday received a wire announcing the death of his brother-in-law, Orah W. Kerner, at his home at Kernersville, N.C.*
>
> *The deceased was the oldest brother of Mrs. Hollomon, who could not be at his bedside on account of the recent illness of her little son and the necessity of taking him to Miami, Fla. after his recovery. They are now in that city for the winter, during the recuperation of little James A. Hollomon, Jr., from severe bronchial trouble, Mr. Hollomon is in Atlanta.*
>
> *The death of Mr. Kerner takes from his section of the state one of its most active and successful young business men. He was president of the American Hosiery Mills, senior member of the firm of Kerner Brothers, merchants, and a large tobacco planter.*
>
> *He was unmarried, and had for twenty-odd years been at the head of the varied Kerner interests. He is survived by his father, two brothers and three sisters.*

As noted earlier, the James A. Hollomon mentioned in the obituary was married to Minnie Gertrude Kerner, sister to Orah and John.

The other Kerner brothers partner was John Glenn Kerner, who served as secretary and treasurer of the company. He died unmarried on March 28, 1951, at the age of seventy-five years.

Northwestern North Carolina Railroad Company

In September 1825, the Stockton & Darlington Railroad Company in England began operation as the first line to carry both goods and passengers on regular schedules using a steam-powered locomotive. The following year, railroad construction began in the United States, and soon after, in 1828, Joseph Caldwell, president of the University of North Carolina, urged the construction of a railroad that would run east to west across the state. However, it was not until 1840 that the first lines opened in North Carolina—the Wilmington & Weldon and the Raleigh & Gaston.

In 1848, the North Carolina legislature finally authorized a railroad to connect the eastern part of the state with the Piedmont. The original plan envisioned construction in four phases. The first, called the North Carolina Railroad, was to serve the Piedmont crescent from Charlotte to Greensboro to Raleigh to Goldsboro. The second, the Western North Carolina Railroad, was to be built from Salisbury to Murphy in the far west of the state. The third phase, called the Atlantic & North Carolina, was to run from Goldsboro to Beaufort and the port at Morehead City. The fourth and final phase was called the Northwestern North Carolina Railroad. This line was to run from Greensboro to the towns of Winston and Salem and then on to Wilkesboro. It was this line that would pass through Kernersville.

The North Carolina Railroad was chartered in 1849, with stockholders forming the company in July 1850. Construction of the 223-mile-long line took five years. It was leased to the Richmond & Danville Railroad in 1871.

The original 1873 Kernersville depot building following its recent restoration. *Photo by authors.*

The city of High Point was laid out in the 1850s as the "highest point" on the North Carolina Railroad and was soon attracting commerce from the surrounding area, including the growing village of Kernersville, according to a notice in the August 8, 1860 edition of the Raleigh, North Carolina *Weekly Standard*:

> *Texas may boast of the first cotton of the season, and South Carolina of her first green corn, but to Kernersville, in old Forsyth, belongs the credit of sending off this year, the first dried blackberries. Mr. J.H. Hester, an enterprising and wide-awake merchant of Kernersville, shipped at this place this week, eight barrels of the above fruit, to Messrs. Stoddard and Clark, of New York.*

The J.H. Hester mentioned in the story was John Henry Hester, a prominent Kernersville businessman who also served as postmaster in the town before and during the Civil War.

The second phase—the Atlantic and North Carolina Railroad—was chartered in 1854, with the state providing two-thirds of the capital. When completed in 1858, it opened ninety-six miles of rail between Goldsboro and Beaufort.

An act to incorporate the Western North Carolina Railroad Company was ratified by the North Carolina legislature on February 15, 1855. It opened in the fall of 1858 with eighty-four miles of line from Salisbury to within four miles of Morganton. In 1875, the state took over the Western North Carolina and operated it until 1880, when it was sold to a local group that immediately resold its interest to owners of the Richmond & Danville Railroad.

In early 1868, a railroad meeting in Forsyth County attended by many prominent businessmen and farmers resolved that the county subscribe $100,000 for an extension of the Northwestern North Carolina Railroad from Greensboro to the twin towns of Winston and Salem and beyond. According to the *Kernersville Bicentennial Book*, local citizens of Kernersville subscribed $10,000 toward this effort. Later that year, the Northwestern North Carolina Railroad Company was incorporated by an ordinance passed March 8, 1868, by the constitutional convention of North Carolina.

Work in the vicinity of Kernersville began in 1868, according to the book *Joseph of Kernersville*. There, it is reported that in May 1868, Philip Körner wrote to two of his children in Indiana that the engineers were surveying the new railroad. Then, in 1870, Körner family records mention that Philip's son, Joseph, a carpenter and contractor by trade, was building a section of the railroad between Kernersville station and the Perry Place about three or four miles west of town and had thirty men working for him. The contract had been awarded to him by Edward Belo, a Salem merchant who had been elected the first president of the Northwestern North Carolina Railroad Company.

Joseph also put his brother Jule to work overseeing the workmen and reported in a letter to his sister, Dora, written in January 1870, that Jule was a "pusher for work." Further reference to the railroad appears in Körner records of 1872, when Joseph wrote to his sister Medora that the railroad would be completed by the end of the year.

Construction of the line to Kernersville is also mentioned in two letters to the editor of the *People's Press* of Salem in 1873. The first, dated February 4, 1873, reads in part:

> *Messrs Editors: The approach of the iron horse is waking up things about our formerly quiet little town. Business is more brisk, and everything is trying to go by steam. We even imagine chanticleer tries to imitate the locomotive whistle in his cock-a-doodle-do. The switch is being laid at the depot, and Dr. Mendenhall has given orders "to surface the road" to this place. A freight train will be run from Greensboro to this place as soon as everything can be arranged.*

> *Your correspondent has been down the road to Greensboro, and finds it smoother than the old* [North Carolina Railroad]. *The rails are connected with "fish-bar-places" which tie them down very solidly. In running, the road has a clear ring, and not the usual "clatter-bang"...Mr. Harmon is pushing the depot to completion. The well is finished and the tank is under construction.*
>
> *Through the influence of Capt Whitten, the train was ordered up, and gave all who wished a free ride to New Garden Meeting-House, where a protracted meeting was in progress...Mr. Jacob Hicks is Engineer, and is careful and attentive to his business...it will not be long before the citizens of Salem and Winston will be on tip toe of expectation, and exclaim, "do you hear the cars?"*

The second letter, in the February 20, 1873 edition of the *People's Press*, added, "The Railroad is completed to this place, or at least, we have seen the smoke and heard the whistle at the depot [and] The Railroad company has sunk a well some 36 feet in circumference at a cost of about $500."

Charles Blacknall Brooks was the first station agent at Kernersville, followed by F.G. Shileut. Shileut was succeeded on December 1, 1873, by

Southern Railway agent Carlton R. Kerner in his office in the depot. Kernersville Bicentennial Book *photo, 1971.*

Richard P. Kerner, who served as freight, passenger and express agent and telegrapher for forty years.

The bicentennial history of Kernersville also records that citizens of past generations remembered the piles of cordwood for the firing of the train, the well near the passenger station and the tanks of water that Cal Kerner kept filled. According to a description there, "The railway depot was built on the north side of the tracks and the single building included office, ticket window, passenger waiting room and freight warehouse. It was framed with peg and mortice [*sic*] timber and the office and waiting room were heated by huge brick fireplaces."

After the Northwestern North Carolina Railroad was completed, trains began to run regularly between Winston and Greensboro. A timetable in the June 15, 1883 edition of the *Kernersville News* gives some idea of the daily schedule at that time:

Leave Salem daily	5:45 a.m.
Ar've Kernersville	6:20 a.m.
L've Greensboro	10:22 a.m.
Ar've Kernersville	11:30 a.m.
Evening Trains Daily, Except Sunday	
Leave Salem	5:40 p.m.
Ar've Kernersville	6:20 p.m.
Leave Greensboro	10:15 p.m.
Ar've Kernersville	11:20 p.m.

While the section from Greensboro to Kernersville was completed by February 1873, construction of the line from Kernersville to Winston and Salem took several more months, and it was not until July 12, 1873, that the first train to traverse the line entered Winston.

The Northwestern North Carolina formally opened for business on August 1, 1873. It was originally constructed to so-called "North Carolina Gauge" (present-day standard gauge), but this was subsequently changed to five-foot gauge to facilitate an interchange with the Richmond & Danville. Eventually, another change was made back to standard gauge.

In 1888, a 74.45-mile extension of the line from Salem to Wilkesboro was commenced, but it did not open until the spring of 1890. On July 24 of that year, the Richmond & Danville signed a ninety-nine-year lease for the now-

Postcard view of the Southern Railway passenger depot at Kernersville that opened for business in 1901. *Courtesy of Wayne Biby.*

completed line. However, the financial panic of the early 1890s swamped the railroad, and within four years it was in receivership. As a result, the company was reorganized in July 1894 by J.P. Morgan as the Southern Railway, which took over the Richmond & Danville's lease. It then operated under the Southern Railway name until August 22, 1894, when Southern purchased the line outright for $250,000. This was followed by the purchase of all the Northwestern North Carolina's capital stock on December 14, 1894. It was the Southern Railway that built the second passenger depot in Kernersville, which opened for business in 1901. It sat on the opposite side of the tracks from the original depot until it was taken down in 1985.

In the early days, train-related accidents were commonplace, and Kernersville was not spared. The *People's Press* of February 7, 1878, recalls one particularly tragic incident that occurred:

> *Mary Ann Meredith, about 40 years of age, daughter of Bradly Meredith, living about a mile below the Kernersville depot, was run over by the train on Saturday morning, the 2nd inst., and killed.*
>
> *It seems, as the train came in sight, running on a down grade, she noticed from the house, as they lived right at the road, one of their pigs on the track, and got over the fence and ran across the track driving it away, when her dress was caught by the cow-catcher, throwing her down, dragging*

her about thirty feet, and leaving her on the road side. Of course the train could not be stopped immediately but as soon as possible the engine was reversed and all haste made to town for a physician for the misfortunate sufferer. But on the arrival of the physician and a number of others life was extinct. She leaves an old father and mother and a little girl who were dependent upon her to some extent at least, (as she received something from the county) towards their support. They are certainly to be pitied, for their main prop is gone.

Under the circumstances no blame can be attached to any one connected with the road. Some said that Capt. Crutchfield looked the very picture of despair when he came back to get help for her.

The train through town provided excitement in other ways as well. These included incidents that grew out of efforts to dodge the conductor to gain a free ride. One example appeared in the *Times* of Richmond, Virginia, on July 10, 1901, under the banner "A Fatal Ridge." According to the story, "While trying to beat his way from Winston to Greensboro last night by riding on the rods of a freight car Cicero Hasten, a young white man, was run over

Photo taken circa 1945 along Railroad Street showing the Southern Railway passenger depot. *Courtesy of the Hull family.*

and killed at Kernersville by falling under the train while trying to dodge the conductor." Another occurrence took place during one of the regular runs of the Southern Railway passenger train on the evening of March 22, 1912. There, a ticketless passenger ordered by the conductor to pay up while on the run from Winston to Kernersville decided to exact his revenge. After leaving the train, he turned and shot the conductor at the Kernersville depot while he was boarding passengers for the trip to Greensboro.

Despite the occasional accident, the railroad service through Kernersville proved a boon to the economy on many levels. It also provided a convenient mode of travel, not only to local destinations like Winston-Salem and Greensboro but also to faraway places across the state and country. However, this golden age of railroad travel did not last. In the 1950s, automobile travel made passenger service to Kernersville uneconomical, and it was discontinued, bringing to a close the era of railroad travel to and from this small town.

Muddy Creek

Kernersville's Earliest House of Worship

One of the earliest Quaker meetings in Piedmont North Carolina was located at Cane Creek in present-day Alamance County. Although it was founded in December 1751, some member certificates date from about 1748, indicating the settlement was already of some standing by the date the meeting was formally established.

In the early 1750s, Quakers began streaming into eastern Guilford County from various meetings in Pennsylvania, Virginia, New Jersey, Maryland and elsewhere. Many carried family names well known in the Kernersville area even today. Examples include Beeson (Beason), Dillon, Stanley, Hiatt and Vestal.

As early as 1751, a meeting for worship was set up at New Garden near present-day Guilford College. It took its name from an earlier New Garden meeting in Chester County, Pennsylvania, as it was often the custom to name new Quaker meetings after earlier ones.

Not long after New Garden Monthly Meeting (MM) was established, Deep River Midweek Meeting was set up in 1753, not far from the current Forsyth County line. Its name came from the nearby stream of that name.

About 1771, a Quaker meeting for worship known as Muddy Creek was established on land that is today within the city limits of Kernersville. It was formally established in 1785 as a Preparative Meeting from Deep River, but by 1818 it was established as Union MM. The records tell us that its original members included Latham Folger and Hannah Hanes, clerks, Thomas Arnett, Asa Barnard, Huldah Barnard, Margaret Barnard,

Benjamin Beeson, Catharine Beeson, John Brooks, Aaron Coffin, Moses Coffin, Sarah Coffin, Job Coggshall, Joseph Crews, Sarah Crews, Asa Folger, Eunice Folger, Matilda Folger, Ezekiel Haisley, Ezekiel Haisley Jr., Joseph Haisley, Mary Haisley, Sarah Haisley, Jonathan Harrold, Margaret Harrold, Susanna Henley, Elizabeth Johnson, Jane Johnson, John Maston, Ann Mendenhall, Elizabeth Mendenhall, Jonathan Mendenhall, Joseph Mendenhall, Martha Nordyke, Mary Patterson, John Pattison, Simmons Pattison, Mary Pike, Nathan Pike, Cadwallader Pitts, Elizabeth Pitts, John Pitts, Hepzabeth Starbuck, Paul Starbuck, Elizabeth Stockton, Daniel Warren, Jemima Weisner, Jesse Weisner, Lydia Weisner, Rebecca Weisner, Gabriel Willits, Priscilla Willits, Lydia Worth, Matilda Worth and Silas Worth. Union was organized in accordance with the following minutes from the Quarterly Meeting:

> *The friends appointed to visit Muddy Creek Preparative Meeting generally attended thereto, and think it best to grant their request* [for permission to hold a MM], *with which this meeting unites and directs said meeting to be held the Fourth day preceding the last Seventh day in each month, and their preparative meeting to be held the Fourth day preceding their Monthly Meeting. Jeremiah Hubbard, Joseph Hunt, Joshua Moore, William Standley, Abel Coffin, Zimri Chase, Samuel Carter and Jesse More, are appointed to attend the opening of said meeting on the 28th day of 1st month, 1818, by the name of Union Monthly Meeting and report their care to the next meeting.*

These minutes were extracted from those of the Quarterly Meeting held at Springfield Friends Meeting (in present-day High Point) on December 18, 1817.

Union MM continued to be held until June 25, 1834, when, as the result of the continuing loss of membership due to the ongoing Quaker migration from North Carolina to the Midwest, it was "laid down," according to Quaker parlance, by direction of the Quarterly Meeting, and the Preparative Meeting was attached to Dover MM. Dover, located near Colfax, in Guilford County, was set up in September 1815 by authority of the New Garden Quarterly Meeting. In fact, a meeting for worship, called Upper Reedy Fork, was established at this location about 1786 by New Garden MM, and the name was changed to Dover in 1793. At the same time that Union MM was

The first Friends meetinghouse at Kernersville, built in 1908. *Courtesy of Mildred Weavil.*

laid down, its property was transferred to Dover, and when that meeting was laid down in 1899, it was transferred to New Garden MM.

The Dover MM property was reported as sold in 1904 in the minutes of New Garden MM, and funds from the sale were used to set up the present-day Kernersville Friends Meeting, which had started with a tent revival in 1906. The first meetinghouse at Kernersville—a simple white-framed structure—was erected in 1908.

It is believed that the Union meetinghouse was dismantled and sold for building materials in the early 1840s. The property where it was located was finally sold to the Whicker family about 1904, and since that time it has been used as a cemetery by the Whicker and Hopkins families.

The Muddy Creek or Union cemetery contains the graves of some of Kernersville's earliest residents. Among those known to be buried there are Abigail (Overman) Pike (born 1709, died February 1781), of whom more will be said presently; Mary Beason (born January 15, 1794, died July 13, 1824); Richard Beason (born 1792, died December 12, 1844); Reuben Folger (born August 23, 1778, died May 22, 1847); William Hastin (Hastings) (born September 5, 1787, died September 10, 1868); David Hendricks (born December 27, 1792, died February 16, 1854); John Henley (born January 26, 1774, died October 25, 1868); Susanna Henley (born April

24, 1780, died August 15, 1856); Elizabeth Masten (born April 21, 1758, died March 30, 1832); John Masten (born March 23, 1761, died March 30, 1832); William Shields (born December 25, 1780, died February 21, 1852); Doughty Stockton (born June 8, 1776, died December 29, 1855); and Elizabeth Stockton (born October 5, 1778, died March 27, 1857). Many of these family names are still to be found in the Kernersville area.

Of these, Abigail (Overman) Pike and her husband, John, were widely known by Friends throughout North Carolina and charter members of Cane Creek MM. Following the death of her husband, Abigail moved to Muddy Creek, where she resided with her son Nathan until her death. She was a minister and felt a leading mission to travel in ministry. According to a *Genealogy of the Lee Family from William Lee of Ireland*, Abigail was quite a lady, as the following passage illustrates:

> [Abigail] *was a minister in the Society of Friends, and was in the habit of riding out to the Army camps* [during the Revolution] *to preach to the soldiers; she was said to be the only minister allowed within the lines, and she was not permitted to dismount, but had to preach from her saddle. Returning one evening with a company of Friends from such a mission, they came to where the road divided, one fork going straight home and the other leading up past the "graveyard;" they were debating which to take; one had remarked that a ghost was to be seen every evening in the graveyard; Abigail whipped up her horse saying, "We will go this way. I have long wanted to see a real ghost, shake hands with it and ask, 'is it well with thee?'" Arriving at the cemetery, sure enough: there it was with arms outstretched; Abigail rode up to it and called back, "Come on Friends, it is only a big cobweb on a bush."*

David Teague, Kernersville native and Quaker historian, was responsible for locating Abigail's grave in the Muddy Creek cemetery, a task complicated by the fact that many of the oldest graves never had more than fieldstones as markers. However, one of the graves was outlined with handmade brick and had what appeared to be a bigger brick sticking upright from the soil in the middle of one of the short sides. A close examination revealed the broken-off stub of a thin, tablet-style headstone on the side opposite the stone, obviously from the foot stone. On it were the letters "A" and "P" in block capitals, with the top part of the "A" and the top right part of the "P" hollowed out. In addition, it was the only grave in the older section of the cemetery to be outlined with the handmade brick and was located very close to other Pike family graves in the cemetery.

It is also of interest to note that the meetinghouse at Muddy Creek has served more than one Kernersville denomination. It is said that after the Quakers left, the meetinghouse was the site of the brush arbor with which Main Street United Methodist Church was started. There seems to be some truth to this because a history of that church states the following: "Since the first Methodists in Kernersville in those early colonial days did not possess a church building, they attended services for several years at the Muddy Creek Meetinghouse, built by the Quakers and located about a mile from the outskirts of the hamlet. Today all that is left of that place is its cemetery."

Just when the Methodists began using the Muddy Creek location is unknown, but it seems certain they were no longer using it by the year 1838, because they had constructed their own church on South Main Street in Kernersville during the period 1837–38 on land donated for that purpose in 1837 by John Frederick Kerner, eldest son of Joseph Kerner.

Bibliography

Government Records

Forsyth County, North Carolina, Deed and Will Records.

Guilford County, North Carolina, Deed Records.

Mecklenburg County, North Carolina, Deed and Will Records.

Pension Application Papers of David Cockerham (S8240), National Archives, Washington, D.C.

Pension Application Papers of John Fields (S8471), National Archives, Washington, D.C.

Pension Application Papers of Michael Fulp (W10043), National Archives, Washington, D.C.

Pension Application Papers of Mary Whicker, widow, (R19003), National Archives, Washington, D.C.

Stokes County, North Carolina, Deed, Will, and County Court Minute Records.

Surry County, North Carolina, Deed Records.

Books

Annual Report of the Bureau of Labor Statistics. Winston, NC: M.I. & J.C. Stewart, Public Printers and Binders. Vol. 9, 1895; vol. 11, 1897; vol. 12, 1898.

Boyd, William K. *History of North Carolina*. Vol. 5. Chicago: Lewis Publishing Company, 1919.

Branson, Levi. *Branson's North Carolina Business Directory*. Raleigh, NC: Branson & Farrar, 1866–67; 1867–68; 1869; 1872; 1877–78; 1884; 1890; and 1896.

Brenaman, J.N. *A History of Virginia Conventions*. Richmond, VA: J.L. Hill Printing Company, 1902.

Coleman, Alan. *Railroads of North Carolina*. Charleston, SC: Arcadia Publishing Company, 2008.

Emerson, Charles. *Chas. Emerson's Tobacco Belt Directory*. Greensboro, NC: Emerson, 1886.

Fries, Adelaide L. *Forsyth. A County on the March*. Chapel Hill: University of North Carolina Press, 1949.

———. *Forsyth County*. Salem, NC: 1898.

———. *Graveyard Register of Friedland Moravian Church, Forsyth County, NC.* Copy from an original made in 1941.

Fries, Adelaide L., and Douglas LeTell. *Records of the Moravians in North Carolina.* Raleigh, NC: State Department of Archives and History, 1954.

Grant, Daniel Lindsey, ed. *Alumni History of the University of North Carolina.* Durham, NC: Christian & King Printing Company, 1924. General Alumni Association of the University of North Carolina.

Guide Book of N.W. North Carolina. Salem, NC: L.V. & E.T. Blum, Printers, 1878.

Haun, Weynette Parks. *North Carolina Revolutionary Army Accounts*. Durham, NC: W.P. Haun, 1988.

Henderson, Archibald. *North Carolina: The Old North State and the New*. Chicago, IL: Lewis Publishing Company, 1941.

Hinshaw, William Wade, and Thomas Worth Marshall. *Encyclopedia of American Quaker Genealogy*. Baltimore, MD: Genealogical Pub., 1969.

Jackson, Donald, and Dorothy Twohig, ed. *The Diaries of George Washington.* Charlottesville: University Press of Virginia, 1979.

Joseph, Edna Harvey, et al. *Genealogy of the Lee Family*. Original 1950 manuscript in Library of Earlham College, Indiana. Microfilm copy made by the Genealogical Society of Utah, 1988 from original.

Kernersville Bicentennial Book, Kernersville, NC: [s.n], 1971, revised and republished 1976.

Kirk, J.S., Walter A. Cutter and Thomas W. Morse. *Emergency Relief in North Carolina: A Record of the Development and the Activities of the North Carolina*

Emergency Relief Administration, 1932–1935. Raleigh, NC: Edwards & Broughton, 1936.

Körner, Jules Gilmer, Jr. *Joseph of Kernersville*. Durham, NC: Seeman Printery, Inc., 1958.

Lefler, Hugh Talmage, and Albert Ray Newsome. *North Carolina; The History of a Southern State.* Chapel Hill: University of North Carolina, 1973.

Magi, Aldo P., and Richard Walsner, eds. *Thomas Wolfe Interviewed: 1929–1938*. Baton Rouge: Louisiana State University Press, 2002.

Matthews, Albert, ed. *Journal of William Loughton Smith: 1790–1791*. Cambridge, MA: University Press, 1917.

Merrill, Samuel. *Newspaper Libel: A Handbook for the Press*. Boston: Ticknor, 1888.

The North Carolina Yearbook. Raleigh, NC: *News and Observer*, 1901–1941 [not published 1917–1921]. Variant title: *North Carolina Year Book and Business Directory*.

Pettengill's Newspaper Director and Advertisers' Hand-Book for 1877. New York: S.M. Peggengill & Co., Publishers, 1877.

Powell, William Steven, ed. *Dictionary of North Carolina Biography*. Vol. 5. Chapel Hill: University of North Carolina Press, 1994.

Reichel, Levin Theodore. *The Moravians in North Carolina: An Authentic History*. Salem, NC: O.A. Keehln, 1857.

Robbins, David Peter. *Descriptive Sketch of Winston-Salem*. Winston, NC: Sentinel Job Print, 1888.

Siewers, Charles Nathaniel. *Forsyth County: Economic and Social*. New Bern, NC: O.G. Dunn, Printer, 1924.

Stanley, Donald W. *Forsyth County Cemetery Records*. Winston-Salem, NC: Hunter Publishing Company, 1977.

State Board of Agriculture. *North Carolina and Its Resources*. Winston, NC: M.I. & J.C. Stewart, Public Printers and Binders, 1896.

Stroupe, Vernon S. *Post Offices and Postmasters of North Carolina: Colonial to USPS*. Charlotte: North Carolina Postal History Society, 1996.

Surratt, Jerry L. *Gottlieb Schober of Salem: Discipleship and Ecumenical Vision in an Early Moravian Town*. Macon, GA: Mercer UP, 1983.

Taylor, Gwynne Stephens. *From Frontier to Factory: An Architectural History of Forsyth County*. Raleigh: North Carolina Department of Cultural Resources, Division of Archives and History, 1981.

Taylor, Jerry L., and Sarah F. Larrimore, eds. *Kernersville High School Remembered: 1927–1962*. Kernersville, NC: privately published by the Kernersville High School Alumni Association, 2002.

Tyler, Lyon G. *Men of Mark in Virginia*. Vol. 3. Washington, D.C.: Men of Mark Publishing Company, 1907.

Walsh's Winston-Salem Business Directories for 1902, 1904/1905, 1906. Charleston, SC: Walsh Directory Company.

Weeks, Stephen B., ed. *Index to the Colonial and State Records: of North Carolina Covering Volumes 1–25*. Goldsboro, NC: Nash, 1909.

Wells, Agnes Mosley, Virginia Gentry Phillips and Carol Leonard Snow. *Joseph Winston: His Entry Book, Surry County, NC Land Entries, 1778–1781*. Mount Airy, NC: A.M. Wells, 1987.

Wevodau, Edward N. *Abstracts of Lancaster County, PA Deed Records (Books R–U) including areas now comprising Dauphin and Lebanon Counties, 1774–1789*. Apollo, PA: Closson, 2002.

NEWSPAPERS

Bee, Danville, VA

Burlington Daily Times, Burlington, NC

Constitution, Atlanta, GA

Daily Herald, Brownsville, TX

Forsyth Liberal, Kernersville, NC

Forsyth News, Kernersville, NC

Greensboro Daily News, Greensboro, NC

Greensboro Patriot, Greensboro, NC

Greensboro Record, Greensboro, NC

Landmark, Statesville, NC

Leader, Kernersville, NC

News, Kernersville, NC

News, Miami, FL

News & Farm, Kernersville, NC

New York Times, New York

People's News, Kernersville, NC

People's Press, Salem, NC

Silver Advocate, Kernersville, NC

Times Dispatch, Richmond, VA
Washington Post, Washington, D.C.
Washington Times, Washington, D.C.
Weekly Standard, Raleigh, NC
Western Democrat, Charlotte, NC
Western Sentinel, Winston-Salem, NC
Winston-Salem Journal, Winston-Salem, NC
Winston-Salem Journal and Sentinel, Winston-Salem, NC

PERIODICALS

Fibre and Fabric 30, no. 768 (November 18, 1899).
Telephone Magazine 24 (October 1904).
Vatter, Fred J. "Timber Shades Bonlee's History." *Chatham County Line* (Spring 2003).

E-MAIL

Bumgarner, Matt. E-mail of July 11, 2009, discussing evolution of railroad lines in North Carolina.
Coleman, Alan. E-mail of July 16, 2008, discussing history of Northwestern North Carolina Railroad Company.
———. E-mail of July 13, 2009, same subject.
Porter, Garland Burns, Jr. E-mail of August 30, 2007, discussing Reverend William Porter of Kernersville and his son, Garland Burns Porter Sr.
Porter, Lee M. E-mail of September 2, 2007, discussing Garland Burns Porter Sr. and his friendship with author Thomas Wolfe of North Carolina.
Sears, Robert. E-mail of January 7, 2008, discussing history of Southern Pilgrim College.
Warden, Janelle. E-mail of December 15, 2006, discussing David Morrow related research.

INTERNET SOURCES

"Chronicling America: Historic American Newspapers." Library of Congress, Washington, D.C. chroniclingamerica.loc.gov.

"History of Main Street Methodist Church, Kernersville, North Carolina." www.mainstreetumc.org/pdf/history.pdf.

Jarvinen, Brian R. (retired). "Storm Tides in Twelve Tropical Cyclones (including Four Intense New England Hurricanes)." National Hurricane Center. www.aoml.noaa.gov/hrd/Landsea/12Tides.pdf.

Phillips, Laura W.W. "Nomination of S.J. Nissen Building, Forsyth County, North Carolina, to National Register of Historic Places, August 28, 2007." www.hpo.ncdcr.gov/nr/FY0753.pdf.

Sanborn Fire Insurance Maps of Kernersville. Sanborn Map Company. North Carolina Maps, University of North Carolina Library. www.lib.unc.edu/dc/ncmaps/?CISOROOT=/ncmaps.

1790–1930 Federal Census Records. Ancestry.com. Generations Network, Inc., 2009. Digital copy of original records in the National Archives, Washington, D.C.

About the Authors

Michael Marshall and Jerry Taylor are both Kernersville natives.

Marshall graduated Phi Beta Kappa from the University of North Carolina–Chapel Hill, where he received both a BS and an MS degree in physics. He is also a graduate of the University of Maryland School of Law. His thirty-three-year professional career as a navy civilian scientist included a dozen years as head of the Navy Laboratory History and Archives Program. He also worked as an assistant to the director of Penn State University's Applied Research Laboratory.

Taylor graduated from the Indiana Institute of Technology with a BS degree in electronics engineering. His career included three years in army electronics, followed by thirty years as an engineer with IBM. Both men have an avid interest in genealogy and local history, and their research has been featured in several newspaper and magazine articles. They are also active in a number of genealogy and local history groups, and both have served on the boards of the Kernersville Historic Preservation Society and the Forsyth County Historical Association. In 2009, they collaborated on their first book for The History Press, *Wicked Kernersville: Rogues, Robbers, Ruffians & Rumrunners*.